MAKING
THE
GRADE

ALSO BY TONY WAGNER

How Schools Change: Lessons from Three Communities
SECOND EDITION

MAKING THE GRADE

REINVENTING AMERICA'S SCHOOLS

TONY WAGNER

ROUTLEDGEFALMER
NEW YORK   LONDON

Published in 2002 by
RoutledgeFalmer
29 West 35th Street
New York, New York 10001

Published in Great Britain by
RoutledgeFalmer
11 New Fetter Lane
London EC4P 4EE

RoutledgeFalmer is an imprint of the Taylor & Francis Group.
Copyright © 2002 by Herbert Appleton Wagner, III

Printed in the United States of America on acid-free paper.

10   9   8   7   6   5   4   3   2   1

Library of Congress Cataloging-in-Publication Data

Wagner, Tony.
Making the grade: reinventing America's schools / by Tony Wagner.
    p. cm.
    Includes bibliographical references.
    ISBN 0–415–92769–2
    1. Education—United States. 2. Educational Change—United States. I. Title.

LA210.W23 2001
370'.973—dc21

2001019898

Where the mind is without fear and the head is held high;

Where knowledge is free;

Where the world has not been broken up into fragments by

narrow domestic walls;

Where words come out from the depth of truth;

Where tireless striving stretches its arms towards perfection;

Where the clear stream of reason has not lost its way into the

dreary desert sand of dead habit;

Where the mind is led forward by thee into ever-widening

thought and action—

Into that heaven of freedom, My Father, let my country awake.

Rabindranath Tagore, "Gitanjali 35"

CONTENTS

FOREWORD

As the new superintendent of Federal Way, Washington, in the mid-1990s, I was desperate for good advice. Spending twenty years in the private sector had given me some experience in attempting to create high-performance systems in a variety of sectors, but how would these lessons apply to education? The teachers' strike during my first two weeks on the job had provided an unexpected opportunity to listen to the concerns and often deep-seated visceral pain of hundreds of teachers, parents, and community members. Fortunately, Rudy Crew, the Tacoma superintendent, was just across Commencement Bay.

Rudy urged me to begin a conversation about the importance of focusing on improving learning for *all* students. Efficacy, specifically the belief that all students can and should learn more than had previously been expected of them, was central to his agenda in Tacoma. Rudy made his case based on the demands of a knowledge-based society, an understanding of how people learn, and a commitment to social justice. Second, Rudy urged me to clarify roles and responsibilities. He drew two intersecting circles on the back of a napkin. In one circle he wrote "What" and in the other circle he wrote "How." He explained that the superintendent's role was to lead a community conversation about what students need to know and be able to do and, with the local school board, to clarify the purpose and goals of education. With a few clear goals, Rudy encouraged latitude in terms of "how" they would accomplish shared goals. And finally, Rudy told me to send teams to the Harvard Institute for School Leadership, a two-week intensive training program that develops leadership skills in both schools and districts. He explained that high expectations for a more diverse group of students, new technologies, and growing market pressures all made educational leadership more important than ever.

After our first teams returned from the summer program at Harvard, an assistant superintendent said, "Don't take this the wrong way, but this guy from the Harvard Institute talks about the same things that you do but in a way that makes sense." Soon after, we invited "this guy," Tony Wagner, to our district for the first of many visits. Tony would visit once a quarter for five days. Each visit began and ended with an hour with the district management team. In between he visited about a dozen schools, where he would listen to focus groups of students, faculty members, and parents and consult to building leaders. Every session was directed by probing questions. He never gave us "the answer"—that we had to construct for ourselves.

Amid the myriad business consulting firms, from the Big Five to the boutique, there is a growing trend for executives and management teams to enlist a "performance coach." These twenty-first-century gurus are one-third strategist, one-third whole-systems-improvement facilitator, and one-third psychotherapist. Tony pioneered the work of performance coach in education and remains one of a small handful of consultants capable of engaging large systems in thoughtful improvement efforts. Fortunately, Tony and his colleagues have now begun to train other performance coaches in the Change Leadership Group at the Harvard Graduate School of Education—a new education consulting enterprise that develops "best practices" for helping schools and districts to improve. Rudy's back-of-the-napkin drawings and Tony's questions remain central to my understanding of this enterprise of education: high expectations for all students, schools as the unit of coherence and change, and the importance of adult learning and leadership.

The education agenda of the Bill & Melinda Gates Foundation is based on these three simple but powerful ideas. Like Tony, we believe that the basic design of American schools, especially large secondary schools, is obsolete. Many schools do what they were designed to do better than ever before, but they are falling far short of meeting new demands. Large high schools and junior high schools were never designed to help all students, but today we expect every student to achieve. The forces of obsolescence—high expectations for all students, more diverse students, information abundance, and market pressures—require schools to step back and consider what they need to do differently or better to help all students achieve. We believe that teachers must be engaged as architects around proven design principles, with a clear theory of change and skilled technical assistance.

In 1944, Irish poet Louis MacNiece wrote about the changing landscape:

> . . . each of us has known mutations of the mind
> where the world jumped and what had been a plan dissolved
> and rivers gushed from what had seemed a pool.
> For every static world that you or I impose
> On the real one must crack at times,
> And new patterns from new disorders
> Open like a rose.

His words were prophetic for education at the dawn of the twenty-first century. The static world imposed eighty years ago has cracked and new patterns are emerging. Some of these patterns from new disorders are promising, others less so. This book outlines how the world has changed, it summarizes what we know about good schools—schools that help all students achieve—and it redirects leaders with productive and provocative advice. This book is an important work for teachers, parents, administrators, and policy makers alike. With guidance from friendly critics like Tony, we have the opportunity to design more humane and effective schools, schools that work for all students.

Thomas Vander Ark,
Executive Director
Bill & Melinda Gates Foundation Education Initiative

ACKNOWLEDGMENTS

A BOOK like this, while the product of hours of solitary labor, is never purely a solo effort. Many people have contributed enormously to the ideas that have gone into this book, and it would be impossible to name them all.

My colleagues at the Harvard Graduate School of Education—Robert Kegan, Lisa Lahey, Richard Elmore, Clifford Baden, Linda Greyser, Evangeline Stefanakis, and Bob Schwartz—have all enriched my thinking and supported my work in various ways, as has Paul Hill at the University of Washington. Genet Jeanjean and Elena De Mur have been, and continue to be, wonderful to work with at Harvard, as well. Associates at the Institute for Responsive Education—Don Davies, Amy Marx, Scott Thompson, Abby Weiss, and Karen Mapp—were also helpful. Finally, a number of school, community, and foundation leaders with whom I have collaborated over the years have contributed to my understanding of essential issues in education: Anne Reenstierna, Judy Guild, Richard Silverman, Jim Gaylord, Frank Herstek, Sushma Store, Kristen Sterling, Sarah Kass, Ann Connolly Tolkoff, Mary Ellen Steele-Pierce, Michael Ward, Mark Peters, Tom Murphy, Mike Nelson, Jill Burnes, Carla Jackson, Sue Burge, John Cornwell, Greg Dike, Pat Gootee, Claudia Weigel, Bob Reily, Ben and Barbara Johnson. Nancy Peltz-Paget, Hilary Pennington, Michael Timpeme, Michael O'Keefe, Warren Chapman, Michele Cahill, and all my colleagues at the Aspen Institute Workshop on High School. They have also provided outstanding models of courageous, committed, and competent leadership.

Several education "pioneers" have greatly influenced my thinking and have also responded most helpfully to my writing and so deserve special mention. Indeed, this book would not have been written were it not for the work of Ted Sizer and Deborah Meier. Anthony Alvarado, Elaine Fink, Richard DeLorenzo, and Roger Erskine also read all or portions of this manuscript and commented most helpfully. All continue to offer both inspiration and intellectual leadership to the task of reinventing schools.

Additionally, several "thought partners" in my life have contributed significantly to the development of my ideas in recent years. They have also offered invaluable comments on this manuscript. Tom Vander Ark is one of the most committed and visionary thinkers I know in education and philanthropy. And Kirsten Olson Lanier is a profoundly thoughtful observer of the education scene and a gifted writer. I am deeply grateful to both of them. Judith Garnier has also been a wonderful collaborator and offered helpful comments on both my work in schools and this manuscript.

I also wish to acknowledge the support of Linda Hollick, Routledge vice president and publisher. When she first read a draft of this manuscript, Linda quickly recognized that the potential audience and appeal of this book was far greater than had been envisioned when I first signed a contract. My editor at Routledge, Joe Miranda, has also been helpful, and Deirdre Mullane did a wonderful job of suggesting many ways to make the manuscript more user-friendly.

Finally, this book could not have been written without the strong day-to-day support, encouragement, and thoughtful feedback of my wonderful wife, PJ Blankenhorn. When I disappear into my study for hours at a time on a weekend—or even on Christmas Eve day, as I am now—she understands and supports me in my work. She knows that I did not merely want to write this book. I had to.

INTRODUCTION:
WHAT'S REALLY WRONG WITH OUR SCHOOLS?

I HAVE worked in education for thirty years—as a teacher, principal, university professor, consultant, founding board member of a charter school, and head of several nonprofit organizations working with schools. For the past twelve years, I have both studied and facilitated the change process in numerous schools and districts in the United States and internationally. I spend most of my weeks working in schools and with various groups concerned about education. Now at the dawn of a new century, as I survey the state of American public education, I find both great reason for hope, as well as reason for serious concern—but my concerns are not those that you may be reading about in the newspapers every day.

What I find hopeful is that we seem to have reached a rare consensus: we must greatly improve the education of *all* young people. This commitment to providing higher quality and more equitable education opportunities for every child in America represents a historic moment—one that could be compared to the agreement to abolish slavery or grant women equal rights.

I also find hope in the exciting work being done by some extraordinary educators around the country. In the last decade, many hundreds of new public schools have been created where the overwhelming majority of students—even those from disadvantaged backgrounds—enjoy a high-quality education—substantially better than the one I received as an adolescent in the "best" private schools. We now know how to educate *all* students to high academic and citizenship standards, as well as how to inspire curiosity and love of learning along the way. We will discover more about the accomplishments of some remarkable educators and the schools they've created in the coming chapters.

However, we will also see that the work of these educators is often ignored, misunderstood, and not supported by educational leaders and policy makers. For while there is agreement on the basic goal of raising the achievement of all students, most people are confused about what's really wrong with our schools, why large numbers of students seem to be doing so poorly, and what it will take to solve the problem.

Hence my first concern: if we do not create a better-informed understanding of the real difficulties related to improving public education, I fear that policy makers will sell themselves and the voting public on a "quick fix" for education that does not deliver results—yet again! And when the schools do not get better quickly, public interest will likely wane. Thus, the commitment to improve education for all students may come unraveled in the midst of impatient and unrealistic demands for rapid results. The erosion of support for public education would be disastrous for many students and for our society.

I also fear a failure of nerve. The kinds of changes needed to ensure that all students achieve at high levels are far more radical than what is generally being discussed by "experts" and policy makers. There is no quick or cheap fix when it comes to providing a high-quality public education for all students.

Finally, I am deeply concerned that many of the new education accountability systems that have been put into place by states in the last five years are having an effect that is exactly the opposite of what was intended. Instead of creating incentives to improve our schools and raise the levels of student achievement, some are, in fact, unintentionally undermining the efforts of many of our best educators to make our schools more effective. They are also turning kids off to learning.

In this introduction, I will explore what I believe to be the real challenges we face in our efforts to improve education—ones seldom discussed in the media or in public forums. Many say they want better schools, for example, but rarely is there any real discussion of what we mean by "better." "Teach them the basics" is practically a battle cry in many communities, but just what *are* the basics today? Are they the same as they were one hundred years ago, when all high school students were required to study Greek and Latin, for example? Obviously not, but when you ask people just what they mean by "the basics," as I have, their answers have very little to do with what is currently being tested on new state exams, as we will see.

Even less frequently do I hear any conversation about the bigger questions. What's really wrong with our schools? How do we know—what's the evidence? And if there is something really wrong, then how did things get this way? As is so often the case in "can-do" America, and especially in education, we are headlong in the pursuit of answers to questions that we haven't even asked. We are busy implementing solutions to problems that we neither fully understand nor agree on. We are operating on untested assumptions or perhaps even myths.

Yet, if we do not have some real understanding and agreement about what the problem is with our schools and what we want our students to learn, then we are very unlikely to move forward. Indeed, many thoughtful observers believe that we have made no significant progress toward improving student achievement in the last fifteen years, despite hundreds of new laws and regulations and billions of dollars of new expenditures. Perhaps the confusion I observe is one explanation. As Albert Einstein said, "the formulation of the problem is often more essential than the solution."

For all of these reasons, I believe we must stop and reflect on some basic questions: What's *really* wrong with our schools? How do our proposed solutions address the problems? Are current efforts to improve education working? If not, why not, and what more might be required?

"SCHOOLS ARE FAILING"

Since the 1983 publication of the famous indictment of American public education, *A Nation at Risk*, authored by the National Commission on Excellence in Education, hardly a day has gone by without some reference to our "failing schools" in the media or in politicians' pronouncements. The belief is widespread that students' levels of achievement are much lower than ever, that most teachers are substandard and mainly motivated by the desire for more money, and so on. In short, the prevailing view is that our public education system has changed for the worse and that it is now a disaster. That's the problem, pure and simple.

But what's the evidence? Falling test scores? Which tests? Many decry the decline in the national average score on the Scholastic Aptitude Test (SAT) since the mid-1960s, but Richard Rothstein's recent careful look at the history of the SAT suggests that what small decline there has been in the last forty years is primarily explained by the far greater numbers and diversity of students taking the test.[1] The SAT is no longer a test taken mainly by a few white males attending elite high schools and hoping to enroll in an Ivy League college—which was the case when the test average was established in 1941.

As I write this book, SAT scores are once again in the news, not because they are falling but because the average math score for students taking the SAT in 1999 was the highest in thirty years!

What about other tests? Again, Rothstein analyzes the scores from the National Assessment of Educational Progress (NAEP), a series of U.S. Department of Education–sponsored tests first administered in early 1970s, and he finds that test scores have actually *risen* for all students at all grade levels in reading and math over the past twenty years. (During this same time, there were small declines in writing and science tests.)

Meanwhile, back in the schools, there is a great deal of evidence to indicate that the American system of public education is doing an incrementally better job than ever before. More students are taking advanced courses in high school, and the number of students who graduate and attend college continues to rise every year. According to the latest Census Bureau data, 83.4 percent of Americans age twenty-five and older have high school diplomas, up from 24.5 percent in 1940, when such data were first tabulated, and from 77.6 percent in 1999.[2]

Then there is the economy. Back in 1983, the reason we were told we were "a nation at risk" was because our public school students were not learning the skills needed for our businesses to remain competitive in the emerging global economy. The argument then was that we had a weak economy because we had weak schools. But now that we have the strongest economy in the world and have recently enjoyed the greatest period of growth in our history, why is it that no one credits the education system?

In fact, there is very little reliable evidence that our system of public education is "failing" and many indications that the system is functioning better than ever. There is no question that we have some absolutely abysmal schools in this country that ought to have been closed down long ago. In New York City alone, there are thirty high schools that have graduation rates of 25 percent or less. But they are not worse than ever. They are the same as they have always been—which is a different problem.

Why, then, all this talk about "failure" and "reform"? Harvard lecturer Paul Revelle has a very interesting interpretation. Revelle, who has been a school improvement advocate for many years, served on the Massachusetts State Board of Education from 1991 to 1996. He observes that the "school reform" battle is more of an ideological struggle than it would appear on the surface and tells the story of how the Massachusetts State Board was taken over by social conservatives. The prevailing view in Massachusetts now is one advocated by what he calls the "pricklies." "They think every problem in public education is the result of the excesses of the 1960s," he said. And so, naturally, the solution is to try to return to the schools of the 1950s. But as we soon will see, the public schools of the 1950s simply did not work for large numbers of students in this country.

Am I saying that there is no problem—that things in our public schools are fine? Absolutely not! I am saying that we have defined the problem incorrectly. The problem is not the "failure" of our public schools. They are incrementally better than they were fifty years ago. They haven't *really* changed—for the better or the worse. The world has. That's the real problem.

"FAILURE" VERSUS OBSOLESCENCE

Just a semantic difference? I don't think so. Defining the problem as "failure" suggests that someone is to blame—which is, of course, exactly what's happening in our society. It is widely assumed that if schools are failing, then educators must be at fault.

The result I see in schools is profound demoralization among teachers. They feel castigated and victimized by the public. Feeling blamed without cause, some strike back. The dialogue—either real or imagined—goes something like this: the high school English teachers say to middle school teachers, "How can I teach kids to write an essay if you haven't taught them to write a good paragraph?" And then the middle school teachers turn around and tell the elementary teachers, "I can't teach these kids to write a decent paragraph if you haven't even taught them how to write in complete sentences!"

But many teachers agree on one thing, and national polls suggest that many Americans do as well: It's the parents' fault. Parents are not doing an adequate job of raising their children, many feel. And so educators often tell themselves, "If only they'd give me kids who were ready for school and motivated to learn, then I could teach them."

The "shame-and-blame" game goes on in schools and communities. And on and on and on. The result is that the people who most need to be working together for the benefit of children—educators and parents—are often feeling more and more isolated, disheartened, and at odds with one another. And misdiagnosing the problem as "failure" has another serious consequence, as well. We're pursuing the wrong solutions—solutions that, I believe, make some of the more deep-seated problems even worse.

These days, the proposed solution to the problem of "failing schools" is very simply stated: mandate more "accountability" for students. If students' levels of academic achievement are too low, then we should "raise the bar" for promotion from one grade to the next and for graduation from high school. The way in which we ensure compliance with these new "high standards" is to create more tests—and more consequences for doing poorly on the new tests.

In the past ten years, every state has implemented new and more rigorous standardized tests for all public school students, and thirty-eight states use these tests to rate their schools. Nearly one half of all states also now have, or will soon implement, an exam that students must pass in order to graduate from high school.

The goal of having academic standards, which are well defined, rigorous, and meaningfully assessed, is very important—and one that I support. But in the past five years, the standards movement has degenerated into the "standardized testing movement." We are only just beginning to understand how serious the potentially negative consequences of this move to ever more testing are for both students and teachers.

Most state standardized tests are the simple, multiple-choice, pencil-in-the-circles kind that we've always had—sometimes with a writing sample thrown in. And because there's been no real discussion of what's most important for students to know and be able to do today, these tests cover more material than ever. There's something in these tests for every subject content expert and interest group, as we shall see in chapter 2. So the idea of rigorous standards has, in practice, come to mean merely imposing high-stakes tests, which require more memorization than ever before.

Thus we find a curriculum that is increasingly a mile wide and an inch deep in most schools. For example, every fourth grader in Virginia must memorize all of the elements in chemistry for the state science exam—a test that must be passed in order for students to be promoted to the next grade. A demanding task, but is it intellectually rigorous or even useful information to an elementary student? By contrast, I wonder how many students can demonstrate that they know what the scientific method is—in my view a more useful and rigorous standard, but one that cannot be tested on a cheap, computer-scored exam. We could find examples like this from many states.

Because each state is developing its own test, the states have to give national standardized tests, as well, in order to be able to compare results with other states. Then there are the tests the federal government administers. Finally, if the new Republican administration has its way, as now seems likely, every single state will be required to administer reading and math tests to every public school student in grades 3–8, in order to receive any federal education funding. Thus the number of hours taken up with test-taking in most schools has risen geometrically and will likely continue to spiral out of control.

But it's not just the hours spent on the tests themselves. It's the weeks and months spent preparing for them that have become a growing burden on schools. Because failure on many of these tests has very serious consequences—for example, not being promoted to the next grade level or not receiving a high school diploma—both teachers and students are desperate to improve scores. More and more, there is only one real class being taught in American public schools: test prep.

It is true that this increased anxiety has led to greater efforts to improve the achievement levels of *all* students and that there is now more discussion about new teaching techniques going on in schools. I documented these positive consequences of the standards movement in the second edition of my book *How Schools Change*. But these efforts and good intentions have yet to produce results. In Massachusetts, for example, large numbers of students—about 45 percent based on current trends—are likely to fail the new state tenth-grade tests, which become a requirement for graduation in 2003. A disproportionate percentage of the students failing the tests are minorities. In 1999, 83 percent of the tenth-grade Hispanic students failed some portion of the test and 80 percent of the African-American students failed, according to a University of Massachusetts study.[3] The results of the spring 2000 tests showed little change.

A growing number of scholars are concerned about the unintended consequence of an increased emphasis on high-stakes testing. Recently, the Civil Rights Project at Harvard University commissioned a series of studies on the educational and social implications of high-stakes testing policies. Some of their findings, as reported by project codirectors Gary Orfield and Johanna Wald in a recent *Nation* article, are very sobering:[4]

- High-stakes testing attached to grade promotion and high school graduation led to increased dropout rates, particularly for minority students.
- Using tests to retain students in the same grade produces no lasting educational benefits.
- High-stakes tests narrow the curriculum by encouraging a "teach-to-the-test" approach in the classroom.

In Texas, a state that has had high-stakes tests in place longer than any other state, Boston College professor Walter Haney's research documents a significant increase in the dropout rate among minorities as a result of high-stakes testing.[5] And a recent study by the Rand Corporation shows that while scores on the Texas state tests have gone up, scores on other national exams like the SAT and NAEP have either remained the same or have gone down. The Rand Corporation study concluded that "these 'stark differences' in performance raised 'serious questions' about the credibility of the state test as a meaningful gauge of academic progress." The report also found that the achievement gap between white and minority students in Texas grew on the national test from 1994 to 1998, even as it narrowed on state test results.[6]

The impact on teachers is equally serious. Having to spend virtually all of their time preparing students for the new tests, many feel they are being asked to do things that are wrong for kids—or to undertake tasks that are impossible to accomplish in schools as they are currently organized.

"I'm desperately trying to teach my special ed students advanced math so they can pass the new state regents tests this spring," one highly talented and committed math teacher recently told me. "But the kids are constantly complaining that they will never use this stuff. And you know what? They're right. What I should be teaching them is applied math. None of these kids know how to balance a checkbook or fill out a tax form. Their welding and shop teachers tell me they don't even know how to measure correctly. And they'll never learn these skills so long as I have to prepare them for the new state tests."

The head of a middle school English department recently confided, "I used to love teaching, and now I hate it. I'm staying until seven or eight at night—and still taking work home. But it's not getting the job done. Some of these kids come to me in seventh grade barely speaking English. And the state expects me to teach all 140 of them how to write a coherent essay by May? It's crazy!"

Many students—especially poor kids in inner city schools—are resigned and hostile. "Why should I care whether I get a diploma?" a tenth-grader challenged me. "I don't have any money to go to college, so what good is the piece of paper?" His friend said, "I could do better on those tests, but you know what? I don't feel like making this school look good. What's this school done for me?"

These comments are not exceptional. They reflect the sentiments of many teachers and students, especially at the middle and high school level. And these problems are not unique to inner-city schools. Even in our best suburban schools, students and their parents are rebelling from state accountability systems where standardized state test scores appear to be all that matter. Don't test well—too bad. Love of learning—it's not on the test. Effort—it doesn't count in the final score. Independent research and project-based learning—no time for that. And, as we shall see, a host of subjects that are very important for success in adult life aren't a part of the curriculum at all.

I think there is growing evidence that states' efforts to increase educational "accountability"—narrowly defined as more high-stakes, multiple-choice tests—may, in fact, be undermining both teachers' and students' motivations to learn new things and achieve at higher levels. It is also threatening long-term parent support for school reform, as the number who are concerned about the excessive amount of testing and the consequences of their children not passing continues to grow. Finally, the intensive focus on testing means that there is no time for a more reflective dialogue about what is most important for students to know and be able to do in our society today.

If we continue down this path, I think it is likely that our schools will get worse, not better. Ironically, the proposed solution to "failing" schools has, in fact, become part of the problem.

So if schools are not "failing" because they are doing about as well as they have ever done, and current "reform" efforts are creating a "test-prep" curriculum that demoralizes students and teachers and causes increased anxiety among parents, where does that leave us? In desperate need, I think, of a different view of the problem and the solutions. The problem is *not* that schools are failing. Rather, the American system of education has become *obsolete*. No one is to blame, but we all share some responsibility for finding the solution.

"REFORM" VERSUS REINVENTION

Just as we found that the word "failure" is an inaccurate and even damaging label for the issues in public education today, the same is true of the universally used phrase "education reform" as the label for the solution.

Our system of public education is more than one hundred years old. It was "invented" in response to profound changes in our society: the shift from a rural, agrarian economy to one that was rapidly becoming both urban and industrial. At the same time, America was opening its doors to large numbers of immigrants from around the world. We needed something more than an unregulated system of one-room schoolhouses—we needed an "assembly-line" form of education that would standardize the delivery of basic skills—the three "Rs"—to large numbers of students. While the current call for "education reform" implies that our schools were once doing a significantly better job than they are now, all we have ever done—or tried to do—was give a majority of students a very basic education—at about a sixth-grade level.

Some of us who went to public school thirty or forty years ago and remember being challenged and having classmates who wanted to learn and achieve forget a critical fact. Our public schools are sorting machines—by design. Kids have always been "tracked" according to perceived ability—as measured by standardized tests—in most public schools in this country. We rarely saw the kids in other tracks or those who dropped out.

And, indeed, we can still find lots of students in college or honors tracks in grades 7–12 whose teachers challenge them and who achieve at levels comparable to the best students in any country. Things have not changed for the worse for this group. What has happened, though, is that the kids who drop out or who are in other tracks or other schools are no longer as invisible as they once were. These students are more visible because they are being left behind in the new economy.

The high school graduation rate for whites was 90.5 percent in 1997, but only 82 percent of African-American youth and 66.7 percent of Latinos graduated. According to a recently completed study by the Education Trust, the gap in skills among those who graduate from high schools is equally severe: 45 percent of white youth can learn from specialized reading materials and understand complicated information. The percentage of Latinos and African

American twelfth-graders with these skills is about 20 percent. The gaps in writing and math skills are comparable—with nearly twice as many whites as minorities scoring at the advanced levels in both areas.[7]

But this achievement gap will not be fixed by simply instituting a tougher test. Historically, our schools have never provided equal opportunities to the poor and minority populations in this country. Both their school facilities and their teachers have always been inferior to those that middle-class white children enjoyed. That's part of what the civil rights movement was about and what the 1954 *Brown vs. Board of Education* Supreme Court decision attempted to redress. Although progress has been made in the past forty years, the "education gap" today still exists and now has far more serious consequences for students who are not getting a quality education.

So, given this history, what does the call for "education reform" mean? What are we supposed to "re-form" our schools to?

In some respects, it isn't just Paul Reville's "pricklies" who long to return to the 1950s. The majority of adults today are deeply concerned about both the pace and the substance of change in our society and its impact on the young. There is a growing sense that the moral fabric of our society is coming unraveled. In researching issues of greatest concern to Americans in the 2000 national election, the nonpartisan Public Agenda Foundation found that 77 percent of all Americans listed "the problems of raising children in today's culture" and 71 percent mentioned "moral standards in this country" as extremely important.[8]

When the public talks about "education reform," they are at least as concerned about values as they are about academics. Interesting evidence for this interpretation comes from an unexpected and largely unexplored finding of a Public Agenda Foundation Study, *First Things First*. They discovered that while large numbers of Americans wanted higher academic standards in public schools, 71 percent of all Americans believe that teaching values is more important than teaching academics![9] We'll explore this issue of values further in chapter 2.

I have discovered through hundreds of focus groups that many local business and community leaders share the broader public's concern about values. They are also concerned about a set of traits they frequently call "life skills." Many who work with the young today are worried about an apparent lack of a "work ethic." Today's youth appear less motivated by traditional incentives than previous generations were.

In a recent study, both college professors and employers were asked how they viewed today's high school graduates. Poor writing skills were mentioned as the area of greatest deficiency—by about 80 percent of both groups. But the other major areas where both employers and professors ranked students as being poorly prepared included work habits, motivation, curiosity, and respect. These are qualities of the heart that have far more to do with motivation and the treatment of others than with preparation in academic subject content areas.[10]

Beneath the broad umbrella of what is called "education reform" we find that different groups have specific concerns—but all have in some way to do with the impact of change on our society and on the young. Yes, adults want all students to master the basics, but they are equally concerned about students' values and motivation for work and learning. Many also now realize that in today's economy the level and quality of one's education is more important than ever and so are committed to providing equal educational opportunities for all students.

What more and more Americans will soon come to discover is that current education reform efforts do not address many of their deepest concerns about our schools. Because of the increased emphasis on passing high-stakes tests, schools do not have time to teach much that is not on the tests. Nor is there time to worry about the increasing minority dropout rate or the apparent apathy of young people—made worse by all the emphasis on tests. Worst of all, the tests results tell us very little about the qualities of mind and heart that matter most for success and happiness in adult life.

The use of the word "reform" is a distraction. Our goal should not be to return to the past somehow—even if it were possible. Our challenge is in dealing with the future. Indeed, the tug of war over school "reform" in this country today may, in reality, be a struggle between those who believe that the best way to deal with change is to cling to remnants of the past and those who eagerly embrace the future.

But that is a false choice. In fact, we have no choice. We must face the new challenges that change brings to education, while strengthening those values and institutions that are most important to us. Today's school reform efforts do neither. The goal of this book is to bring these disparate needs and values into sharper focus and a new alignment.

We have a new problem in American public schools, and most people have no real idea how it will be solved or even the dimensions of the difficulty: we must make sure that *all* students have both the skills and values they need for work and citizenship in a rapidly changing world. We must motivate *all* students to want to achieve higher standards, both intellectually and morally, despite the growing influence of an amoral popular culture that encourages consumption, not creation.

Motivation is a critical issue for those who work in schools as well. Feeling victimized and unappreciated by the language of "failing schools," many of the best teachers and administrators talk of leaving the profession.

Many others are reluctant to take risks or work more collaboratively for change and need new kinds of support and incentives. A recent front-page *New York Times* article documented the chronic shortage of individuals willing to be school principals. With all the added stresses of "school reform," increasing numbers are leaving the job, and it is getting harder and harder to find replacements.[11]

The current wave of "education reform" is not providing positive incentives for either student or adult learning. For the most part, it is test driven and punitive minded. The central task we face is not to *reform* American public education, but to *reinvent* it—just as we had to do nearly one hundred years ago. To begin this process, we must stop the senseless pursuit of facile answers, like more and more testing, and begin a thoughtful dialogue around a few important questions.

In the succeeding chapters, I pose what I believe to be the most urgent questions related to the reinvention of public education at the dawn of a new century. My goal is not to offer all the answers, but rather to provide a framework and some starting points for this inquiry and reappraisal, one that parents, educators, and community leaders may find useful. I believe that we must all consider together the following questions:

- What should *all* high school graduates know and be able to do? What does it mean to be an educated adult in America today? Should schools teach values? And most importantly, who should be making these important decisions? These are some of the questions we explore in chapter 2.

- What about testing and assessment? How do we hold students, teachers, and schools accountable? In chapter 3, we look at some of the best ways to gauge student learning and hold schools accountable for results.

- How do we motivate all students to want to achieve at higher levels in a world that is more demanding and confusing than ever? What should the schools of the future look like? And how do we motivate educators and other adults to work together in new ways to create them? Chapter 4 offers a consideration of these questions.

- And, finally, in chapter 5, we turn to the question of what kinds of leadership we need in order to move forward. We will look at some shared responsibilities of politicians, business and community leaders, citizens, educators, and parents in helping to improve our schools, and we will learn more about new models of educational leadership.

Throughout the book, I also relate some of the experiences of individuals and groups whose pioneering efforts point to fresh answers to these questions—education programs that are working for all students and places where educators come to work every day excited rather than demoralized.

The shape of the future of American public education can be found in a number of new small schools around the country. What we learn from their successes will surprise many: the schools of the twenty-first century need to be much more like the schools of the nineteenth century than our present bureaucratic, "factory-model" schools—with the important exception of technology. I call these schools "New Village Schools," and I explore how they work and what kinds of incentives and accountability systems they need in order to flourish.

But before we look at these new schools, we first need to understand the broader context for change in education—the fundamental transformations that have taken place in our society and what they mean for today's students, teachers, and parents.

1

HOW HAS THE WORLD
CHANGED FOR CHILDREN?

LIVING in the midst of rapid change, most of us have a hard time truly seeing its essential features. But if we are to understand more deeply what students need to know and be able to do, as well as what kind of schools will be most helpful to them, then we must first consider how a changing world is shaping today's young people and their future.

In teacher and community forums around the country, I have often asked audiences to reflect on how our world has changed in the last quarter century or so. People's first response is frequently—"everything!" Everything, that is, except schools. Schools probably have changed less than any other institution in our society. Did you know, for example, that the unit of study used in almost all American high schools today—called the Carnegie Unit—was introduced in 1906? It determines how the overwhelming majority of teachers and students spend their days in school, and it is still the way we organize information that is sent to colleges. Is there one other thing invented at the turn of the last century that remains in daily use in this country by millions of people that has changed so little?

But just saying that everything has changed except schools doesn't get us very far in deepening our understanding of what must be done to improve them. We have to look further, and to do so we need a framework that will help us order and make sense of all the change around us. In my work with parents, educators, and community leaders, for some time now I have discussed the important changes we need to understand in four broad categories:

- Work
- Learning
- Citizenship
- Motivation for learning

This is not meant to be a complete list or categorization of all changes, but rather a way to capture those that are critical to our understanding of education for the twenty-first century. Most who've used this framework have found it very helpful.

WORK

When our system of education was invented a hundred years or so ago, most people in this country earned their living with their hands—at first, mainly on farms and then on assembly lines. For most of the last century, the vast majority of work in this country required very little or no formal education—beyond the ability to follow the boss's orders and show up for work on time. Even as late as 1960, only about 20 percent of all jobs in this country required any kind of training beyond high school.

But in a very short period of time, all that has changed. We have moved from an industrial, assembly-line economy to one that is increasingly dominated by technology, information, and service—and the pace of change in this direction is accelerating rapidly. The skills required in this new economy are radically different. "Smart hands" are no longer good enough. Today one has to have both intellectual and social skills in order to get a decent job.

A number of studies have described the skills now needed for work in our rapidly changing economy. Harvard's Richard Murnane and Frank Levy from M.I.T. perhaps best summarize this consensus in their book *Teaching the New Basic Skills*. They document a fundamental change in what employers now expect their workers to know and be able to do for both blue- and white-collar work and explain "the new basic skills" now needed to get a decent-paying job:

> Over the last decade, more and more businesses have begun to look for a similar kind of worker. In addition to things that employers have always looked for—reliability, a positive attitude, and a willingness to work hard—these employers now look for hard and soft skills that applicants wouldn't have needed 20 years ago:
>
> - The ability to read at the ninth-grade level or higher
> - The ability of do math at the ninth-grade level or higher
> - The ability to solve semi-structured problems where hypotheses must be formed and tested
> - The ability to work in groups with persons of various backgrounds
> - The ability to communicate effectively, both orally and in writing
> - The ability to use personal computers to carry out simple tasks like word processing

Murnane and Levy go on to observe, "A surprise in the list of New Basic Skills is the importance of soft skills. The skills are called 'soft' because they are not easily measured on standardized tests. Today, more than ever, good firms expect employees to raise performance continually by learning from each other through written and oral communication and by group problem solving."[1]

In the groundbreaking and well-researched book *Emotional Intelligence*, Daniel Goleman comes to a similar conclusion. He finds that what he calls "EQ"—the capacity for self-awareness, self-regulation, motivation, empathy, and social skills—is much more of a determinant of adult success in work and in relationships than IQ is. And the authors of both books observe that there is no correlation between high IQ scores and EQ or mastery of soft skills.

The implications of these economic changes for education are profound: *all* students must now learn *new* skills. Let's consider each part of this new problem.

All Students

Historically, as I've mentioned, American public schools—especially our high schools—have been sorting machines. We have always sorted out—or tracked—the small percentage of students who were going on to college and have given them a more rigorous education. The remainder—perhaps 80 percent—got just bare-bones schooling, which was all that was needed in the old economy. Now, however, we have to teach *all students* "higher-order" thinking skills—such as how to form hypotheses and solve problems—if they are to be employable. We must also teach all students how to use new technologies.

But we don't yet know how to educate all students to these higher standards, nor do we know how to teach all students how to use new technologies. We've never had to do it before.

New Skills

In elementary schools, children are taught to treat each other nicely, but these efforts are a far cry from what is now needed. As the work of the previously cited authors makes clear, students today must have EQ or soft skills to be successful in work—the ability to communicate effectively with different kinds of people and work in teams, for example.

We do not know how to teach these skills, nor do we know how to assess them. We've never had to do it before.

This analysis makes even more clear, I think, why the educational problem we face is reinvention, not reform.

Murnane and Levy and a growing number of economists are concerned that more and more jobs in the "new economy" require skills that high school graduates simply don't have. While the percentage of the population that has earned a B.A. degree has stayed nearly the same for the past thirty years—about one-third—the number of jobs that require further learning has shot up dramatically. According to Stephen Rose, senior economist at the Educational Testing Service, "You need a bachelor's degree just to apply for the best jobs. That is as it should be for doctors, lawyers, scientists, engineers, computer specialists. But look at middle level managers. In 1960, only 40 percent had a bachelor's degree and today it is 80 percent."[2]

The only jobs left over for students with no more than a high school education are those that require virtually no skills—and which pay next to nothing. According to Murnane and Levy, between 1979 and 1993, the average annual wages of high school graduates dropped from about $28,000 to less than $20,000, while college graduates' wages stayed about the same (as expressed in 1993 dollars). Since 1993, all wages have increased during a prolonged period of economic growth. However, the wage gap between those who only have a high school diploma versus a B.A. degree has actually *widened*. According to the Economic Policy Institute, in 1999 the average hourly wage for high school graduates was $11.83, while college graduates were earning nearly double—$20.58.[3]

The need for a better-prepared workforce has, in fact, been the driving impetus of school reform since the early 1980s, not new research about learning. The primary reason given for the need to improve our schools is economic: the argument is that we need more highly skilled workers in a highly competitive global economy.

School reform, then, has been "business-driven." Corporate CEOs like IBM's Lewis Gerstner have led the national school reform efforts and lobbied for higher standards and accompanying tests. In many cities, it is the business leaders who are pushing hardest for significant change in schools. Indeed, corporate leaders organized all three of the national Education Summits that took place in the past decade, and educators were not even invited to the first two!

Many educators are disturbed by the increased focus on workplace skills in schools. They fear that corporate leaders are dictating what should happen in education and believe that it is not the role of schools to prepare students for work.

I disagree. First, the skills needed for work and for higher education are now essentially the same. To prepare students for work is not simply to give them a vocational education—such as learning how to weld, for example. Preparing students for work today means developing the skills of independent learning, problem solving, and teamwork, as we have seen. In fact, business leaders say they do not want schools to teach students a particular set of skills, fearing that new technology will quickly make specific skills obsolete.

The second reason we must think about preparation for work is to ensure that all students have equal access to economic opportunities in this country. It is a matter of ensuring greater economic democracy. If we look more carefully at the consequences of students not having real skills, we begin to understand how urgent our task is. Gone forever are the days when a high school graduate could go to work on an assembly line and expect to earn a middle-class standard of living. Students who leave high school today without skills and unprepared for further learning are unlikely to ever earn enough to raise a family—let alone buy a house. They are being sentenced to a lifetime of poverty. A generation's future is at stake.

LEARNING

What Must Be Learned

At the heart of the new economy is the transition to what many call "the information age." The implications for education of the explosion of information and its increasing availability are as profound as the economic changes to which these changes are tied.

When the modern high school curriculum as we know it was introduced in 1906, we were an information-scarce society. Many towns did not yet have a library, and very few families had anything like encyclopedias in their home. Thus, only a very small number of people had easy access to information that they might need. If, for example, you wanted to know the capital of Nebraska, it was not something you could easily look up somewhere. And a hundred years ago, knowledge was also more stable or enduring than it is now. For the most part, what was learned in most academic subjects in 1906 was still true ten years later. At the turn of the twentieth century, then, memorization as a means for learning made some sense. It was the only way to retain common knowledge one might need later, and the knowledge retained was likely to remain useful over time.

Today, neither of these things is true. Instead of information scarcity, we have information glut—and the information is constantly new and

changing. It is now commonly believed that the amount of stored information is *doubling* every five years, and most of it is almost as available as
tap water.

In a very few years, the Internet has dramatically changed the information
"problem" in learning. It's as if children were suddenly given a 500-million-
channel cable TV but no TV guide! The problem today is no longer access to
information. The real challenge is how to filter and make sense of all the
information that bombards us daily. Reasoning skills are more important
than ever as we try to sort out both what is true and what is important from
the overwhelming amount of data available online.

Not only do we have far more information, but it is also constantly changing. Almost daily, it seems that shifting political contexts, increasing
globalization, rapid advances in technologies, and new discoveries in all the
sciences quickly alter what we think to be true. Addressing this information
revolution, former Harvard University president Neil Rudenstine noted
that "the 'half life' of what is learned in the humanities is eight or ten years,
and in math and the sciences it is three or four."

What all this means for schools is that the dominant learning "technology" of the past one hundred years—textbook-based instruction and tests
based on memorization of facts—is hopelessly obsolete. Many textbooks are
out of date before they ever even get into classrooms. Once in place, they are
often used for a decade or more before schools can afford to replace them.

It is true that you can walk into most classrooms in this country and find
a computer or two in a corner—or an entire computer lab in a separate
room. But these appearances are deceiving. In most of our public schools,
there aren't enough computers to go around, they are usually very slow and
out-of-date, and they are not connected to the Internet. Even in wealthy
school districts, where computers are newer, more plentiful, and connected, computers are seldom used in classrooms. Teachers haven't been
trained in how to integrate them into the curriculum—or are uncertain
about giving up their role as the "expert."

In the new information age, the concept of the teacher as the sole repos-
itory of knowledge is as obsolete as the textbooks, but even under the best
of circumstances, learning new teaching methods is a challenging task for an
aging teaching force. And our circumstances are hardly the best. Many studies have shown that what little money is available for teachers' professional
development in public schools is often squandered on "one-shot" programs
that have little connection to the most urgent challenges related to improving teaching and learning.

How Learning Happens

The need to develop new methods of teaching becomes all the more urgent as we better understand how children learn. The approach to teaching in our public schools for the past one hundred years has been heavily influenced by behaviorism, the dominant school of psychology for much of the twentieth century. Behavioral psychologists have assumed that children are empty vessels when it came to learning, mere repositories for whatever they were taught, and so educators knew very little about the internal learning processes in students. It appeared not to matter what they were thinking, or whether they thought at all, as long as the teacher had the right combination of rewards and punishments.

Today we know that, in the words of Swiss psychologist Jean Piaget, "to understand is to invent." A growing body of accumulated research undertaken by both educational practitioners and developmental psychologists points to a new and very different understanding of the child and the learning process. The work of Maria Montessori, John Dewey, Jean Piaget, Lev Vygotsky, and the current work of Howard Gardner has in common a view of the learner as one who is driven to discover by an intrinsic need to make sense of the world.

Real learning happens at every age through a dynamic interaction between the student, his or her prior experiences and understandings, and new experiences or information. If a lesson is not organized around a student's inner activity of learning, then what is learned is superficial or fleeting. Often, even very gifted students do not really understand material they have supposedly learned in school.

Howard Gardner, in his book *The Unschooled Mind*, describes experiments with students from elite universities who had memorized the definitions of scientific and mathematical laws for gravity, motion, and so on, but who could not explain what they meant. More serious still, when these students were presented with phenomena in a laboratory that the theories were meant to explain, the students didn't invoke the theories, but rather reverted to childlike explanations of the occurrences. Gardner describes comparable misconceptions and examples of reversions to stereotypical thinking in the humanities and social sciences as well.[4]

In other words, very able students could repeat a memorized law, but they could not apply it. Gardner and other developmental psychologists and educators now know that the only way students come to a deeper understanding of abstractions such as these is by having opportunities to "construct" new knowledge through a more active process of developing questions, formulating hypotheses, and carefully observing the results of hands-on experimentation. This is what Piaget meant when he said that understanding comes through inventing.

In my own teaching experience with both adolescents and adults, I find that students develop a much deeper understanding of a problem—say the need for school reform—when they first consider the data and formulate and debate alternative interpretations prior to my offering a point of view. I begin all of my classes, workshops, and even keynote talks by asking an open-ended question and giving time for small-group discussion. The process of having to struggle to make meaning of a work of art or a contemporary issue generates new insights and a much deeper understanding than would occur if I simply presented my interpretation without time for collaborative inquiry.

Demanding that students pose questions, actively sort through data, and develop, test, and refine hypotheses through dialogue and critical inquiry is often referred to as a "constructivist" approach to learning. Students are, literally, constructing new knowledge, with regular coaching from the teacher. Teaching students in this more "constructivist" manner requires both greater skill and more time. Developing the skills and creating the conditions in schools for this approach to teaching and learning are part of the problem of reinvention and represent a significant challenge. Some will ask if it is worth the effort and expense. Many adults believe that rote learning served them well enough when they went to school. Why is anything different needed now?

The answer, of course, is that those were different times. These new methods of teaching are not just another educational fad. They are the only way to develop the reasoning and problem-solving skills needed in the workplace and the analytic capacities required to make sense of the ocean of information we find ourselves flooded by today.

We might also keep in mind that the teaching methods described here are not new, though the theory may be. While memorization has always had and will continue to have a role in education, for thousands of years the elites in most societies traditionally have been taught through a more active process of inquiry and dialogue. Indeed, one might say that the inventor of the Socratic dialogue, Socrates, was the first constructivist educator. The Chinese have long understood the power of a more hands-on approach to learning as well. They have a very old proverb that goes something like this: "I hear and I forget. I see and I remember. I do and I understand."

For much of this century, a growing chorus of progressive educators has talked about the need to create teaching methods that are consistent with the research about how children learn. But often this call has gone unheeded because it is much easier to test students' retention of facts than to determine whether they have a deep understanding of a scientific or mathematical concept. This is a problem that we shall discuss at greater length in the next chapter.

In summary, while school reform efforts are predominantly "business-driven," as we have discussed, changes in the nature of work are a necessary, but insufficient, reason for rethinking public education. New research about how children learn is also an important reason to revamp our curricula and methods of teaching. But this focus also leaves several issues critical to the future of education unaddressed. There are two other categories of change that provide a powerful impetus for education reinvention, and they are rarely, if ever, mentioned by either business or education leaders. One is the increased need for citizens in our democracy to be well-informed and active members of their community. It is this issue to which we now turn.

CITIZENSHIP

Critical Thinking

Democracy as a form of government requires citizens to be informed about the issues in order to be able to vote intelligently. That's the main reason Thomas Jefferson and other founding fathers advocated strongly for a free and universally available system of public education. We have always believed that schools should prepare students to be citizens in a democracy. This has not changed in more than two hundred years, though the topic gets scant attention in the media.

For much of the past century, we prepared young people to be citizens by requiring some kind of semester-long high school civics course. The curriculum for these courses mostly covered the structures of our democratic forms of governance: the respective powers of the executive, legislative, and judicial branches of government and the powers of local, state, and national government. Additionally, required American history courses taught students about our important founding documents, such as the Constitution.

At the turn of the last century, the task of preparing students for informed citizenship was a great deal simpler than now, but this curriculum remains unchanged today, for the most part. It may have served in 1920, but it is no longer sufficient now. I agree with those who are concerned about high school graduates' lack of knowledge of the Bill of Rights and other important information about our system of government, but their inability to think critically and their lack of civic participation are of far greater concern to me.

In many ways, the history of the twentieth century is an account of the increasing threats to human survival and challenges to our established beliefs. As a result, citizens must understand and respond to issues of ever-increasing complexity. New weapons that can destroy the planet in a matter of minutes make decisions about issues of war and peace infinitely more serious. New technologies that have the capacity to create or take away or alter life enormously complicate thinking about both policy and moral issues. The threats to our environment posed by technology and industrialization are without precedent. The increasing economic and ecological interdependence of countries blurs boundaries and forces us to think in new ways about the meaning of nationalism.

Clearly, the nature of these and other challenges today requires future citizens to know more than just the history of American government and how it works. Students need to be taught how to think critically about the major issues of our time—and those that are likely to be of concern in the future. They must learn to analyze data as they struggle to understand problems. They need to understand the difference between reasoned argument and ideology, sift through conflicting claims, and come to their own informed opinions. Finally, tomorrow's citizens should know how to express their views clearly and concisely, both in speech and in writing.

Political Engagement

As important as these skills are, they will be of little value if citizens are not involved in government and civic affairs. A democracy requires a population that both understands the issues and votes. Here the trends in our country are deeply disturbing. Robert Putnam's new and important book *Bowling Alone* chronicles the decline in political and civic participation in America.

Putnam's data show a drastic decline over the past forty years in the percentage of eligible voters who turn out on Election Day. In 1960, about 63 percent of voting-age Americans cast ballots for president. By 1996, the number had dropped to about 49 percent—by far the poorest turnout of any democracy, except for Switzerland. (The data from the 2000 election show about a 2 percent increase—probably because the presidential race was perceived to be so close.) This sharp drop is despite the substantial *increase* in the percentage of African-American voters in the South who now vote as a result of the civil rights gains in the 1960s and the passage of the 1965 Voting Rights Act.[5] According to Putnam, "Outside the South, the slide in electoral participation since 1960 is, by now, the longest decline in American history, and voting in the 1996 and 1998 elections was substantially lower than in any other presidential and off-year elections in nearly two centuries."

Who is to blame for this growing crisis in our democracy? Pundits point fingers in different directions. Everything from the media's "instant" predications of winners to American's growing distaste for all politicians and despair about the political process gets mentioned. Few seem to have any ideas for solutions. Surprisingly, almost no one expresses the view that our public schools might have a role in reviving participation in political life, despite the fact that the age group that has the lowest voter turnout is eighteen- to twenty-four-year-olds, at 28 percent.

If students do not learn about the responsibilities of citizenship in school, then where else are these lessons likely to be taught?

Civic Engagement

Alexis de Tocqueville, in his famous study of democracy in America in the early nineteenth century, observed that part of the strength of American democracy is its citizens' willingness to work together in a wide range of voluntary associations. Except for a time in the 1930s during the Great Depression, this trend held true for much of the twentieth century as well—right up until the 1960s.

In *Bowling Alone*, Putnam documents the decline since 1960 of participation in every kind of "face-to-face" civic and social organization in America. While mailing list membership in national nonprofit organizations—such as environmental and civil rights groups—has risen, membership and leadership in organizations where you have to "show up" has plummeted, according to a wide range of indices.

Putnam's analysis of research from "time diaries," for example, reveals that "nearly half of all Americans in the 1960s invested some time each week in clubs and local associations, as compared to less than one-quarter in the 1990s." Other surveys point to even more troubling data about the decline in community leadership. Putnam summarizes these findings: "Between 1973 and 1994 the number of men and women who took *any* leadership role in *any* local organization—from 'old-fashioned' fraternal organizations to new age encounter groups—was sliced by more than 50 percent." In short, "Many Americans continue to claim that we are 'members' of various organizations, but most Americans no longer spend much time in community organizations—we've stopped doing committee work, stopped serving as officers, and stopped going to meetings."

The point here is not to lay blame but to understand the implications of these changes for education and the challenges that we face. Two aspects of this trend have particular importance for schools.

The first is, once again, the generational nature of this decline. As Putnam notes, "Members of any given generation are investing as much time in organizational activity as they ever were, *but each successive generation is investing less*" (my emphasis). I must ask again: If civic participation and community service is not taught in schools, then where will future citizens learn this lesson so essential to a healthy democracy?

The implications of the decline in the number of adult volunteers involved in schools are also critical. Consider the membership statistics of the Parent-Teacher Association (PTA). Growth in local PTAs was explosive through much of the twentieth century, and by the 1960s they represented the largest secular membership organization in the country. Since that peak, membership has plunged from nearly fifty members per one hundred families with children under age eighteen to less than twenty per one hundred today.

Of course, there are many understandable reasons for this decline, the increasing number of hours all Americans now work and the rise in the number of single-parent and dual-career families among them. While many busy families no longer see the point in involving themselves with some of the traditional PTA-type activities such as bake sales, educators must share some of the responsibility for this decline as well. As they have felt attacked and on the defensive, they have more frequently blamed parents for their lack of involvement in schools—thus creating subtle but pervasively unwelcoming climates for parents in many schools today.

The problem is big enough for us all to share some responsibility. My point is not to lay blame. The point is to understand the impact on children's lives and what must be done to improve education. Educators have never been able to take on the task of educating the young all by themselves. And, for a host of reasons, they are even less able to do so today. The diminished involvement of adults in all aspects of school and student life—from PTAs to school boards to youth groups—is a significant part of the education problem that we must address. We cannot possibly educate all students to high standards without greatly increased adult involvement in the education of children—for reasons that we shall soon better understand.

Civility

Less well documented but even more serious—I believe—is the decline in everyday civility in our country. From daytime TV and talk shows whose stock in trade is legitimizing meanness to the growing problem of "road rage" to the strident and angry tone of many town meetings, we seem to be losing our sense of courtesy and decency in America.

The causes are debated endlessly. The loss of a sense of community, frustrations resulting from the frenetic pace of our lives, sheer fatigue from working longer hours—all these and more are mentioned and are significant. But my greatest concern is what is happening—and what should be happening—in our schools. The data I cited in the Introduction—indicating that 71 percent of all Americans believe it is more important to teach values than academics in our public schools—suggest that many share my concern.

Sadly, however, many school communities are a mirror of the problem of incivility, rather than an antidote. School board meetings—instead of being models of civil discourse—have too often become places where citizens come to harangue educators and vent frustrations. Sometimes their grievances are legitimate. Often, however, the individuals who shout the loudest represent a tiny splinter group or fringe element in a community that has come to advocate for or against a particular cause or textbook—often for ideological reasons. Meanwhile, many decent folk stay home, not realizing that fringe groups are often dictating our school policies.

In more communities than I care to count, I have also seen school board members themselves act in ways that set a very poor example. In my book *How Schools Change*, I documented a school board meeting in Cambridge, Massachusetts, where an experienced board member and town elder chastised and humiliated dedicated teachers whose ideas he did not like—and no one, not even the chair of the board, stepped in to stop him. And in my consulting work, I am frequently called in to assist school boards whose members have lost all respect and trust for one another—or who never had it to begin with.

Among faculty, I have also seen personal discourteousness and disrespect go unchallenged. In many schools, one finds that a handful of older teachers are often the de facto leaders—for better or for worse. They outlast principals and superintendents who come and go and so often have more authority with their peers. Sometimes this power is positive—as in cases where veteran teachers lead a change process or mentor new teachers. More often, however, the attacks on education and consequent demoralization of educators described earlier results in a sense of frustration and cynicism among older faculty. Some become bitter and will lash out at any new ideas or proposals for change. Newer or more decent-minded teachers are too often cowed into submission by this psychological bullying. Even principals become intimidated by what they call the "naysayers" and give in to them.

If this behavior is allowed to persist over time and honest dialogue is thwarted, the school culture becomes poisoned. Faculty meetings become a time for announcements and little more. The real conversations often take place in the parking lots—behind people's backs. Gradually, the resulting distrust and lack of respect become so pervasive that teachers are not able to collaborate with one another or agree on anything. Any change or improvement process is paralyzed. Often, my first task as a consultant is to help teachers re-create a climate where honest but respectful dialogue becomes the peer norm.

But I've learned it isn't the adults who suffer most in these dysfunctional schools. It is the students. Several years ago, I received an unexpected call from the superintendent of a highly regarded (and very wealthy) school district in New England—a district whose standardized test scores and college attendance rates were the highest in their state. Much to my surprise, this superintendent needed help. The high school student government had written a public letter to the school board complaining about their teachers. No, it wasn't the grading system or amount of homework that led these students to take this highly unusual step. It was the way their teachers talked about each other in front of the students! The teachers were constantly criticizing or complaining about other teachers in classes. As Ted and Nancy Sizer make very clear, "The students are watching."[6]

An isolated example? Hardly. Before I consult a school or a district, I gather information. Of course I look at the quantitative data—test scores, dropout rates, percentage of students continuing on for further education, and so on. But I also gather qualitative data, as an anthropologist might, to understand the culture of a school or district. Focus groups—small-group discussions with representative samples of different populations or constituents—often give me the most important information, and focus groups with students are especially useful and interesting.

I usually talk to high school students (although conversations with younger students also can be very helpful) and I ask some variation of the same three basic questions: (1) What do you like most about your school? (2) What are some important ways in which it might be improved? and (3) If there was one thing that could be changed in the next year that would make the greatest difference *for your learning*, what would it be?

The answers to the last question are remarkably consistent. In both so-called good and bad schools, in urban, suburban, and rural communities, the most common answer to the question of what students would like to see changed is *relationships*.

In most schools, students say that lack of respect is widespread and is of great concern to them—lack of respect among adults, between adults and students, and among students themselves. But it is teachers' apparent lack of respect for students that most bothers the kids. Even in elite independent schools, students complain about teachers who try to show how bright they are by making certain students the brunt of sarcastic banter and clever put-downs. This humiliation often has lasting emotional consequences for the students who are the teachers' victims.

According to a recent Public Agenda Study, *Getting By: What American Teenagers Really Think about Their Schools*, only 41 percent of all public high school students surveyed felt that most of their teachers respected them. And this is not simply racism—the percentages of students reporting this lack of respect was the same across all racial groups. In this same study, students were also asked what changes in school would likely make the greatest difference in academic achievement. Sixty-nine percent of the students surveyed said that they would learn "a lot more" from a teacher who treats them with respect. And when students were pressed to name the *one change* that would most help them learn more, "having more good teachers" was the overwhelming first choice of more than 60 percent of the students.

We like to think that while the adult world may sometimes be a place where civility is in short supply, at least schools are islands of decency. Sadly, in most schools I visit, this is not true. Schools are too often part of the problem rather than the solution. Students will tell you schools are physically safer than adults commonly believe, but many are not safe places to be emotionally. As any good teacher will tell you, trust and respect are the foundation of active engagement and genuine learning in any classroom. And positive relationships with teachers are even more important to students today, as we shall see.

Positive relationships are equally important for adults who are committed to improving an organization. Collaboration, rooted in trust and respect among committed adults, is the most essential condition for meaningful change in any organization. Without trust and respect, there is no real learning and dialogue about the need for change. Without trust and respect as a school norm, we cannot even begin to consider how to best educate students for citizenship.

We talk a lot about education that improves IQ. Now, thanks to Daniel Goleman's work, we are also talking about EQ, or emotional intelligence. But what about "CQ," the phrase I use to describe "Citizenship Intelligence?" In my view, developing these three human capacities must be at the core of all that we do in schools.

MOTIVATIONS FOR LEARNING

The requirement that all students master more complex thinking and problem-solving skills, the increased importance of soft skills or EQ, the new approaches required to teach for understanding, and now the importance of addressing the issues related to educating for citizenship, or what I call CQ—all of these place new and very intense demands on teachers today. They are what I call the "rock" in the problem equation. But these new requirements of education are only half the problem.

Teachers are caught between this rock and a "hard place" that is little understood by most people who do not work in schools. Cumulative social changes in our society have dramatically affected many students' motivations for learning in several important respects. This is at least as difficult a problem for educators as those that I have already discussed.

Think back a moment to what has traditionally motivated young people to learn. For most, it was some combination of respect for authority and the desire to succeed. And the concept of success was, in turn, connected to the idea of hard work and delayed gratification. I work hard now in the belief that I will have a significantly better life later, when I will enjoy the enhanced fruits of my labors. For many young people today, neither of these motivations have the power that they once had.

Diminished Respect for Authority

It is commonplace for adults today to remark on young people's increased lack of respect for their elders. While this may or may not be true, what is often forgotten is how our attitudes toward all forms of authority have changed radically in the last forty years in America. The civil rights movement, the women's movement, Vietnam, Watergate—all of these events have dramatically impacted the ways in which we see authority in our society today. Gone forever are the days when authority remained unquestioned. Today, anyone in authority has to earn the respect of others—even those over whom he or she has formal authority. It is no longer granted automatically because of a title or position, as in the past.

For the most part, we applaud this progress. We now look to many different people for leadership, and our belief in their abilities is based more on merit than on position. We understand that the best decisions are often made after consultations by all those likely to be affected. Problems are best solved by teams, rather than individuals. And authorities in our lives now must earn respect.

However, when it comes to life in schools, there is a down side to this generally progressive trend. I hear older teachers complain about feeling less respected by students. But the real consequence is that students no longer just do work because the teacher tells them it is important. This problem is made more serious by the sheer size and anonymity of our schools today. If students feel neither known nor cared for by teachers, why should they pay any attention to them?

Then there is the media's role in undermining even rational and respectful authority. If you look at today's most popular youth-oriented films and listen to their music, a dominant theme is defiance of all authority. From movies about the forgotten child left home alone to renegade cop films, the themes are very similar: Adult authority is incompetent.

What about the Parents?

Many people in our society would say that the job of motivating students to do well in school is primarily the responsibility of parents, not teachers. And most parents agree. In a recent study of attitudes toward parental involvement in schools, 83 percent of the parents surveyed said that checking homework and encouraging kids to learn were their most important jobs in relation to school.[7]

However, large numbers of teachers don't believe they are getting the support from parents that they need. Eighty-three percent of the teachers surveyed in the same study said that parents failing to set limits and create a structure at home or failing to control how much time kids spend at the TV, on the computer, and so on was a "serious problem." Parents' refusing to hold kids accountable for their behavior or academic performance was listed by 81 percent of the teachers as a serious problem.

The most startling finding of the study, however, was the number of parents who feel they are not doing the job that needs to be done with their *own children*. Despite the fact that 74 percent of the parents surveyed said they're more involved in their children's education than were their parents, *only 23 percent of parents said they "know a lot about how to motivate their children"* (my emphasis).

Why do so many parents find it increasingly difficult to motivate their children to do homework and succeed in school? The answer, I think, lies in the nature of the very powerful messages being "taught" to children by the media—and in young people's growing disconnect from *all* adults.

Impact of a Consumer-Driven Economy

We decry the violence in the media and worry, as we should, about its impact on the young. We are appropriately concerned about the extent to which young people today are exposed to soft and hardcore pornography. But we appear to take for granted the consequences for children of a culture dedicated to consumption.

Consider the subtle but serious messages children are bombarded with daily: you can buy happiness; you don't have to work for it; why put off until tomorrow what you can buy today; joy is in having, in owning. Add to this the real-life lessons that children are exposed to: parents and relatives who have worked hard all their lives getting laid off on a moment's notice, while others—media personalities, athletes—who don't seem to work at all—have it all.

The belief in nineteenth- and early-twentieth-century Horatio Alger ideals—hard work, perseverance, self-discipline—is eroded or contradicted by powerful media messages to the contrary. Sex and violence? Often, they are not the real message; they are simply tools to increase sales. The real message is: Live to consume!

Yes, some children of materially successful families appear as motivated as ever. Their parents drill them with the idea the good life does not come cheap. These children are taught from an early age that if they wish to maintain the lifestyle they enjoyed while growing up, then they are going to have to work hard and get into a good college and have a well-paying career.

But what about the children who may not have money for college—those who have what I call "TV fantasies" of a fancy career, big house, and a sports car, but who believe the chances of achieving that life are remote? What do they work for, live for? Not learning, not school, not the distant future. Often by the time they are sixteen, they live to buy the late model car they've been eying or to go shopping at the mall on Saturdays to get the latest CD or computer game or hot new outfit. For many in this generation, delayed gratification is something measured in days or months, not years. Delayed gratification means having to work more hours at McDonalds than you want to in order to make next month's car payment or fund your weekend shopping sprees.

Am I saying that this generation is somehow lazier or more decadent than generations past? Absolutely not! I could fill this book with examples of young people's idealism and perseverance at learning and mastering things that interest them. What I am saying is that the culture appears to celebrate passive consumption and instant gratification, and these values have a pervasive effect on young people's motivations for learning. Simply put, the majority of young people today will not work hard in school just because an authority tells them to or because they believe that their hard work will be well-rewarded in five, ten, or twenty years.

They're not "buying" those lines. They're off buying tangible things that do not require long waits or obeying orders. If teachers are to work effectively with all young people today—and not just those from the most success-driven families—they must discover and nurture different motivations for learning than those we've relied on in the past.

The Growing Isolation of the Young

The erosion of traditional respect for authority and the seductions of a consumer society are, of course, things that good teachers, parents, and other adults involved with young people deal with successfully every day. They talk to young people about what is important in adult life, and they are role models for the values they profess. Traditionally, young people have probably always learned life's most important lessons through close relationships with caring adults both in and out of school.

Mihaly Csikszentmihalyi and Reed Larson sum up the importance of these relationships in their classic study, *Being Adolescent*. "In all societies since the beginning of time," they write, "adolescents have learned to become adults by observing, imitating, and interacting with grown-ups around them. The self is shaped and honed by feedback from men and women who already know who they are, and can help the young person find out who he or she is going to be."[8] The problem today, however, is that these adult–young person relationships are becoming scarce in our society. Our children are growing up largely isolated from adults and from the positive relationships with older people that are so important for learning.

Many changes in our society account for this trend. We know that family life has been transformed in just a few decades. As we've already observed, there are many more single-parent and dual-career families. Fewer members of extended families live with their grandchildren, nieces, or nephews. And all adults are working significantly longer hours, according to Juliet Schor's recent study, *The Overworked American*.

Outside of the home, there are many fewer opportunities for young people to interact with adults. Teachers have little time for interaction with students outside of class. Sports and extracurricular activities—where many students have traditionally found connections to teachers—involve fewer students than ever. This is true, in part, because the growing size of schools, combined with budget cuts, allow fewer students opportunities to become involved. Then, too, many young people flee school at the earliest opportunity and opt to work more hours to support their consuming habits instead.

Other adults are also significantly less involved in activities like scouting or Little League. In the community, the chances for adolescents to work alongside adults in formal or informal apprenticeships are also diminished or so altered that they do not provide for the kinds of relationships that make a difference in the life of a young person. Working at the local car wash is not the same as assisting a mechanic in a garage.

Csikszentmihalyi and Larson documented this trend in their study by giving students pagers and asking them to write down what they were doing and with whom when they were paged. The authors produced some very disturbing data. In their analysis of what adolescents do in their waking hours, they discovered that young people spent almost as much time alone, 27 percent of their week, as they did with friends, which was 29 percent. This amount of time spent alone is significantly greater than what is found in other countries, they report.

But the greatest surprise, according to the authors, was how little time teenagers spent in the company of adults. Their findings are critical for understanding how young people are growing up today and the implications for education. Only about 5 percent of adolescents' time was spent with a parent or parents—and a disproportionate amount of that time was with their mothers. One-on-one contact with all other adults combined—teachers, a boss, grandparents, or other relatives—added up to only 1.6 percent of their time.

The conclusion from this data is inescapable: young people today are growing up profoundly alone—perhaps more than at any time in human history. They are being raised by each other, as much as by anyone.

I think it is worth considering whether there is a link between the growing number of school shootings and this isolation adolescents experience. Numerous media accounts suggested that Columbine High School students Erick Harris and Dylan Klebold fell through the cracks of a privileged but frenetic adult lifestyle, and no one appeared to have noticed—not the parents, not the teachers. Is it possible that their killing rampage was a way of being noticed, finally, as well as an act of revenge against an apparently cold and uncaring adult world?

Whether or not this is true, it is undeniable that the cumulative effects on young people and on education and of all the changes that have taken place in the last thirty years are profound, little understood, and rarely discussed. It's easy to talk about "failing schools." It is much harder to hold a mirror to our lives, our culture, and ourselves and consider some of the ways that we, collectively, may be failing our students and teachers. Yet this is what we must do.

The point is not to shift the blame, however, but to learn together. Understanding more fully the changes in our economy, what students need to know and how learning happens, the increased need to educate for all aspects of citizenship, and, most significantly, students' life circumstances and motives for learning is our first shared task.

With a more clear view of the problem, we have a significantly greater chance of finding the right solution. With an understanding of how the world has changed around us, we can make wiser decisions about what is most important for students to know and be able to do and how their work can best be assessed. With a greater sensitivity to the significant pressures both students and educators face today, we can begin to create better schools and more effective methods for bringing them into being.

It is these topics to which we now can turn.

2

WHAT DO TODAY'S STUDENTS
NEED TO KNOW?

THROUGH the ages, communities and cultures have had to decide what is most important for the young to know and be able to do. In earlier times, when issues of survival and transmission of traditional culture and beliefs were the main preoccupation, many of the answers to this question may have been self-evident. Elders taught the young what their elders had been taught before them. The decision of what to teach the young was not often a topic that took a great deal of time or thought.

Now, in an era of information glut and rapid change, we must think very carefully about what we want all children to know, as well as how we can best test, or assess, their expertise. We need to reconsider what it means to be an educated adult in the twenty-first century and make tough decisions among competing priorities. But, thus far, few communities have taken on this most important challenge. They are leaving the task to the test-makers, who, in turn, are deferring to the academic experts and the politicians. So let us look at how our current system answers the question of what all students should know and why.

THE DOMINANCE OF THE ACADEMIC DISCIPLINES

In a quest for higher academic standards in this country for the past fifteen years, we've been asking academic subject experts what students need to know. This overreliance on "experts" has gotten us into very serious trouble in education. If, for example, you ask one historian what is most important for all students to learn, you are going to get a long list of concepts and events. If you turn to his or her colleague and ask the same question, you are going to get another long list. And they won't always agree. And when there has been disagreement within an academic discipline, the tendency has been to accommodate all those involved and include everything that has been advocated.

But it gets worse. Sociologists, geographers, psychologists, anthropologists, political scientists, and others all want a crack at that social studies curriculum, too. Each views his or her academic subject as having content that's vital for students to know. And so The National Council for Social

Studies, the national professional organization that serves as the umbrella organization for these different academic disciplines, produces ever-lengthening lists of knowledge that is "essential" to their discipline. The same is true in many of the other academic subjects. Biologists, physicists, chemists, and earth scientists struggle over the science curriculum, and English teachers are forever debating what great works of literature should be required reading for all students.

The math area may be the most irrational of all. For reasons that escape me, the math academics have decided that all students who go to college should know "advanced math"—as opposed to having more practical skills like how to understand statistics, do measurements, create budgets, and so on. It has become a rigid "gate-keeper" for college entrance. And since we now think all students should have a "college-prep" curriculum, every student is therefore expected to master advanced algebra, plus elements of calculus and trigonometry, in order to receive a high school diploma.

There are many problems with this expert-driven approach. The first is the growing quantity of knowledge that diverse groups are saying students must master. In practice, higher standards have come to mean simply learning more stuff. It is the "add-on" approach to curriculum improvement. Even when the most thoughtful national groups, like the New Standards Project, sit down to create new curriculum frameworks for learning standards across all subjects and all grades, they are still the prisoners of academic content experts. Their high school curriculum content standards—while much more intellectually rigorous than most—nevertheless ends up as a simply overwhelming list of what students are expected to master. Let me offer an example from the subject area that I and most readers will know best—high school English.

In the New Standards high school curriculum, there are seven categories of standards for English. Under just *one* of the seven English categories—literature—*every* student is expected to master, and will be tested on, the following skills:

- Makes thematic connections among literary texts, public discourse, and media
- Evaluates the impact of authors' decisions regarding word choice, style, content, and literary elements
- Analyzes the characteristics of literary forms and genres
- Evaluates literary merit
- Explains the effect of point of view
- Makes inferences and draws conclusions about fictional and nonfictional contexts, events, characters, settings, themes, and styles

- Interprets the effect of literary devices, such as figurative language, allusion, diction, dialogue, description, and symbolism
- Evaluates the stance of a writer in shaping the presentation of a subject
- Interprets ambiguities, subtleties, contradictions, ironies, and nuances
- Understands the role of tone in presenting literature (both fictional and nonfictional)
- Demonstrates how literary works (both fictional and nonfictional) reflect the culture that shaped them

Each of the other six categories of standards in English has a comparable list of expectations. Then there is the requirement that all students will also read twenty-five books a year.

I can tell you that only a few of the best English students whom I taught at Sidwell Friends—one of the most elite private schools in the country—could demonstrate mastery of all these competencies, and very few of them read twenty-five books a year. Further, I would suggest that only the ones who are taking the Advanced Placement English exams or are planning on being English majors in college *need* all of these skills.

And that's just one-seventh of one subject! All of the other subject content areas in the New Standards materials—the different subject areas of mathematics, biology, chemistry, earth science, physics, and so on—have equally long lists of expected outcomes for which teachers and students are supposedly accountable. When you consider that students usually take five academic subjects a year in high school—English, social studies, math, science, and a foreign language—the list of what is expected is totally overwhelming and completely unrealistic.

A much more rational approach would be for specialists from the different but related disciplines to agree on skills or knowledge that are common across several academic subjects. But this doesn't happen either at a national level or in schools. The biology, physics, and chemistry teachers never talk about a common science literacy curriculum, for example. Rarely do the history and English teachers get together to talk about shared standards for teaching research skills or essay writing. And while the New Standards Project has an excellent description of what they call "applied learning standards," mastery of these competencies is expected *in addition* to everything else that's listed.

POLITICS IN THE CURRICULUM

Recognizing that academics may not necessarily be the only or even the best source of knowledge about what students should know, some states hold hearings or establish blue-ribbon commissions to create new state learning standards. But the results are often the same. The former member of the Massachusetts State Board of Education whom we met in the Introduction, Paul Reville, explained what happened there when his group set out to create new state standards in a recent interview: "In 1994, there were a series of high-profile hearings on the new Common Core of Learning—what every high school graduate should know and be able to do. It was a very inclusive process. In fact, one reason why the state learning standards are 'a mile wide and an inch deep' is precisely because the process was so democratic. Everyone's point of view and priority got included."

The Massachusetts experience is typical. Occasionally, though, state school boards will take matters into their own hands and completely disregard the views of academic content experts—with results that are at least as problematic. In the headlines for much of the last several years was the controversy surrounding the Kansas State School Board's decision not to include the teaching of evolution in its new science curriculum standards.

Leaving the newspaper headlines aside and returning to the reality of the classroom, we find that teachers are pressured into covering more and more academic content in their courses. Lacking a consensus about what is most important, everything becomes equally important. So teachers try to cram more into the day, the month, and the year—even though many know that this approach does not encourage deep understanding or real skill development. It is also a way of teaching that leaves many students falling farther and farther behind.

TESTING AS THE CURRICULUM

The push for higher academic standards has added substantially more content to the curriculum in nearly every state. And with the increased push for accountability, states have created standardized tests that assess more and more of this content. The so-called high-standards, high-stakes testing system continues to grow and appears, increasingly, self-perpetuating and out of control. The academics add to the list of what must be taught in each discipline, the test-makers add this content to their exams, which in turn drives the teachers to keep adding more and more material to their courses, in order to be sure that they have covered what might be tested.

Why do we test for so much factual information, when common sense as well as countless studies tell us that facts are quickly forgotten, easily looked up, and are not what's most important to learn?

As we have seen, part of the answer is that communities haven't had the hard conversations about what is most important to learn and so they fall back onto the easy and noncontroversial answers—just the facts, ma'am.

Often when educators advocate for assessment of critical thinking or problem-solving skills, a few conservatives will complain that testing these skills is too subjective and so shouldn't be done at all.

Another major determinant of our system of assessment is money. Most European systems of education rely extensively—often exclusively—on essays and oral exams that test reasoning, applied learning, and problem-solving skills. We do, as well, in some of our advanced Placement high school courses for the most elite students, and no one complains about the subjectivity of the teams of teachers who grade these exams. But such tests are very expensive to create and to score. Each Advanced Placement exam, for example, costs more than $75 per student to administer. By contrast, most standardized, computer-scored tests being used in American public education today cost between $1 and $5 per student.

Political and financial considerations often come together in state decisions about what kind of high-stakes testing program to impose. Once again, Massachusetts is an interesting case study. The State Department of Education's 1994 Five Year Plan stated that "the new assessment system will strive towards a goal of authenticity by incorporating essay, problem solving, and other open ended questions in place of multiple choice." The plan went on to advocate for use of interdisciplinary projects and student portfolios as the best measures of the development of students' skills.[1]

However, this focus was soon lost, according to Reville. The first problem came when the state board learned how expensive it would be to create the kinds of assessments they wanted to use. Not knowing what to do, they turned the problem over to the state education bureaucrats, whose hands were tied by a limited budget for test development.

Then the former president of Boston University and a conservative education critic, John Silber, was appointed chair of the state school board by Governor Weld in November 1995. According to Reville, who was on the board at the time, "Silber demanded plenipotentiary powers and wanted to choose his own board. The board was reduced from 16 to 9, and the new members were all very ideological. They were all outside critics who had never worked inside the system. All they knew how to do was lob grenades."

One of Silber's first grenades was to throw out the work of a group of educators who had been working on the social studies standards. His criticism was that they did not call for enough memorization of facts. And, it turns out, a test of factual recall was far less expensive to develop and score than an essay-based exam.

Massachusetts is hardly unique. In too many states, money and politics are the deciding factors in what gets tested. And what is tested on the cheap, computer-scored, standardized exams is becoming the only real answer to the question of what students should know in America today. The tests drive curriculum and, more and more, determine whether students graduate or are promoted.

These test scores are also used as the yardstick to measure how good schools are, and many families use school district test score averages to decide whether a community is even a desirable place to raise their children. Your local realtor will confirm that real estate prices are heavily determined by the perceived quality of schools—which, in turn, is measured by standardized test scores. Often, prospective buyers with children will ask about a community's test scores before they even go look at a house. Thus, cheap, computer-scored tests have come to be a significant determinant of real estate values, as well as what our children are taught.

What about College?

The reason increasing numbers of parents look at a community's test scores before making a decision about where to buy a house is because they want their children to be well prepared for a "good" college. Teachers also often give this as the primary reason for teaching academic courses that require a great deal of memorization. The perception of what the "good" colleges expect in terms of test scores and academic preparation is a driving force for many education decisions in middle-class communities and so deserves consideration.

It is true that test scores and grade point averages are still important considerations in the college admissions process in state schools, where admissions staffs are spread too thin to consider other more subjective factors. But admissions officers for the "name brand" colleges will tell you that these quantifiable indicators account for only about half of all factors in their decision making.

Equally important to Ivy League admissions committees is evidence of students' leadership, curiosity, and capacity for independent learning. Selective colleges are looking for evidence of mastery of the same soft skills Murnane and Levy found essential in today's workplace, as we've seen. And they also understand the importance of emotional intelligence. As we will see in the next chapter, schools whose students test poorly but who, nevertheless, have very high academic standards and assess these "new basics," are quite successful in getting better colleges to disregard test score data altogether and look at other indicators of student achievement instead.

But given the high college dropout rates in this country—more than 50 percentage of all students who start college never finish—the more relevant question parents and teachers should be asking is: What does it take to stay in college and do well? Here the answers will surprise you.

Several years ago, I conducted a two-hour focus group with a representative set of students who had graduated three to five years previously from one of the leading public high schools in New England—a school that sent more than 90 percent of its graduates on to college. My first question was how they perceived the strengths of their high school. Students talked about a number of things they considered to be positive elements of their high school experience: the many opportunities for participation in extracurricular activities and sports, the fact that the school was quite small, getting along well together, and teachers being available for extra help after school.

After almost an hour of discussion, no one had said a word about classes. And when I asked about academic preparation, the response was immediate. "I didn't remember stuff that was on tests a week after I took them," one student explained. "And it didn't really matter. Except for math, you basically start over in college. They teach you the same stuff all over again."

I went around the circle and checked this answer with the other students—several of whom were enrolled in Ivy League colleges. They all nodded their heads in agreement. I then asked how some of that high school class time might be used to greater advantage—what they might have learned, in other words, that would have enabled them to be better prepared.

"More writing!" several replied. "Study skills," was the next reply. Then someone added, "Learning how to do research." "Knowing how to work in groups," several said.

The list was remarkable—all the more so since theirs was a school known for its excellent writing program.

The students' responses are consistent with data cited in the Introduction from a study of what employers and college professors said were the skills most lacking among employees and college students. It is summarized in the following table:[2]

Skill/Attribute	Employers	Professors
Writing	79%	82%
Work habits	75%	74%
Motivation	71%	59%
Curiosity	55%	54%
Respect	54%	34%

Lack of academic content or preparation, other than poor writing skills, was not a significant concern of either group.

REDEFINING INTELLECTUAL RIGOR: COMPETENCIES VERSUS COVERAGE

The data clearly shows that whether it is preparation for work or for college, the knowledge that matters most today is *not academic subject content. Competency—what you can do with knowledge—matters more than coverage.* In an age of instant access and information overload, mastery of real skills is much more important than memorization.

Although this conclusion is a point of view that many Americans share, as we will see, few leaders seem willing to question the academic status quo. Perhaps it's because they were good students themselves, and so they just assume that what they learned in school are things all students can and should know. Or maybe they, too, are under the spell of the "good college myth" that drives the school concerns of so many middle-class parents. Whatever the reason, state education leaders continue to talk tough about "high standards" for all students and create tests that give teeth to the standards, but they seem to have given very little thought to what students really need to know.

Hugh Price, president of the National Urban League and a leader in school improvement efforts, also has deep concerns about leaders' lack of serious thinking about what new state standards should be. Shortly after the last Governor's Summit on education, he wrote:

> The rush to impose rigorous standards begs the question of where they should be pegged. *It was startling to hear several governors at the National Education summit confess that in their haste to get tough, their states probably had given less thought than they should have to the actual content of the standards.* (my emphasis)
>
> In my view, the standards students are expected to meet should be pegged to the proficiencies that real people need to succeed in the real world. They shouldn't be mirror images of the admissions standards for selective universities.[3]

Price went on to propose "six clusters of competence," which he believes all students must master before leaving high school. These recommendations have recently been adopted by Education Program of the Bill & Melinda Gates Foundation—the largest educational grant-making program in the world—as recommendations for goals that districts and schools might consider.[4] According to these standards, all high school graduates should be:

- *Literate*: Capable of demonstrating a working command of reading, writing, and speaking in English.
- *Mathematically competent*: A command of the basic computational skills required in the modern workplace and in everyday adult life.

- *Problem solvers*: Eager to seek out information, discover answers, and apply their skills in reasoning and critical thinking to solving problems.
- *Scientifically literate*: Capable of appreciating nature and the environment, familiar with the scientific method and the role of science in modern life, and cognizant of the uncertainties of the scientific method.
- *Good citizens*: Well grounded in the forces and values that have shaped this nation historically, culturally, demographically, politically, and economically with an appreciation for the relationship of the United States to the rest of the world and this country's role in the world.
- *Technologically advanced*: Comfortable with technology and capable of using computers and related technologies in the normal course of everyday work and learning.

This list of competencies implies a new definition of intellectual rigor that should be made explicit. Competencies are not mere skills. Knowing how to punctuate a sentence correctly is a skill. The ability to write clearly and logically is a competence. I would also argue that determining what's worth writing about is part of the competency of being a good writer.

The goal of competency makes clear that the aim of education is not the ability to acquire and retain information—the traditional formulation. Nor is it a subjective or "feel-good" philosophy like "love of learning" or even "critical thinking—terms so-called progressive educators sometimes use. I believe that framing education goals as the ability *to do something with what you know*—to apply information in the search for a solution to a problem or to create new knowledge—creates an expectation of more rigorous forms of accountability and assessment, as we will see in the next chapter. It may also be a way of getting past some very old arguments, which in my view have clouded the conversation about the goals of education.

The Problem of Ideologies and Education

So-called education conservatives and progressives have been debating what's most important to learn for most of the century. And, as we saw in the Massachusetts story, when one group gains significant power, they are able to shape the curriculum of hundreds of thousands of children. So we need to look briefly at some of the parameters of the debate and find a more rational course.

Some conservatives claim that if teaching and testing competencies become the focus of the curriculum, traditional academic subject content will no longer be taught. But you cannot teach writing or critical thinking or research or the scientific method without academic content. You have to have something to research, to hypothesize, and to write *about*. A competency-based curriculum can only be built upon a solid foundation of content knowledge.

Second, educators who use the "constructivist" approach to teaching described in the first chapter are not saying that all knowledge has to be "discovered" to be valid and that memorization has no place in the curriculum. Personally, I'm very glad I've memorized my times tables in math and know how to figure out restaurant tips without having to resort to a calculator.

At the heart of the constructivist argument is the question of the motivation for learning—an issue we discussed briefly in the last chapter and to which we will return in chapter 4. There is empirical evidence about the circumstances under which students do and do not retain factual information. Unless the information is connected in some way to the interests or needs of the learner, it, quite literally, goes in one ear and out the other. True intellectual rigor and relevance for the learner are inseparable.

Finally, there is the question of what E. D. Hirsch calls "cultural literacy." He believes that there is a core body of knowledge—factual information—which all students must know in our society in order to understand many aspects of our inherited culture and form of governance.[5]

I believe this argument has some validity. Students need a foundation of knowledge and information for true literacy and lifelong learning. A recent book by Richard Suskind, *A Hope in the Unseen*, describes the struggle of a young African-American student, Cedric, at an M.I.T. summer camp for high school students and later in college at Brown University. Lack of writing skills was his biggest problem. But he also floundered socially when the conversation turned intellectual around the dorm dining table. He had no idea who Freud or Einstein were, for example.

Unfortunately, the issues of the importance of memorization and facts in education are often presented and debated in black-and-white terms. Common sense is a victim of the crossfire. The questions are: What is our focus? What is most important? And what is the relative balance of competencies versus academic content coverage—critical thinking versus memorization of facts—in the curriculum?

The question of what's most important to learn should not be addressed ideologically—by either the liberals or the conservatives, as is too often the case today. It must be considered in light of the changes in our society. What was considered an intellectually rigorous education one hundred years ago is not and should not be the same today. Knowledge of Latin and the ability to read Greek were considered indispensable skills at the turn of the last century, yet few would say these are necessary skills today. Conversely, no education today would be considered rigorous without some knowledge of how to use new technologies for continuous learning.

In other words, discussion of what students need to know and be able to do must be grounded in a thorough understanding of the changes in what is required for work, for lifelong learning, for citizenship, and for personal growth and health. These four categories of change become an indispensable framework for thinking about what it means to be an educated adult in the twenty-first century.

In addition to understanding the competencies most needed today, any discussion of what students need to know and be able to do must be connected to how various competencies will be assessed. In good schools, as we will see in the next chapter, *what* students need to know for graduation and *how* their level of competency will be tested are inseparable.

Thus, my wish list for what all high graduates should know and be able to do is a set of competencies and assessments that are tied to what I think all students will need for future work, lifelong learning, citizenship, and personal growth and health.

Workplace Competencies

- Completing one or more work internships
- Solving a complex problem using teamwork
- Using technology to find, organize, and present information relevant to solving a problem
- Analyzing a problem using statistics, trend data, and probability
- Writing a postgraduate work or study plan and preparing a resume

Competencies for Lifelong Learning

- Presenting, both orally and in writing, an independent research project
- Passing a test on the key features of a geographical map of the world
- Filling out a timeline of important events in history and analyzing an important event in history from multiple points of view
- Demonstrating understanding of the scientific method
- Filling out a 1040 tax form, creating a household budget, and opening a checking account
- Passing second language proficiency test

Citizenship Competencies

- Completing a community service project
- Registering to vote
- Demonstrating an understanding of an important current issue
- Passing a proficiency test on the principles of democratic government

Competencies for Personal Growth and Health

- Completing an independent artistic or musical project
- Demonstrating proficiency in a lifelong sport
- Passing a proficiency test on basic principles of human health

I offer this list to illustrate how student competencies can be connected to the categories of change we discussed in chapter 1, as well as to specific assessments. But I am not advocating this as *the* set of graduation requirements for all students in this country. I do not believe that's my task—or the task of any one individual or group in our society. Which begs the question . . .

WHO SHOULD DECIDE WHAT STUDENTS SHOULD KNOW?

The first most important question in the standards debate is: What should all students know? Equally important is the question: *Who* should be making basic decisions about public education in a democracy? In an age of increasing complexity—and of growing specialization—more and more we tend to defer important decisions to the "specialists." This is both understandable and appropriate in many areas such as medicine and law—but even in these examples, it is important that citizens know the right questions to ask.

But what about education? Who should decide what all students should know? Not the people who have been making the decisions for the last few decades, I have argued. Not academic content specialists. And certainly not politicians or test-makers. What's the alternative? Can ordinary citizens and educators, working together, make wise decisions about what's important to learn?

For most of the last century, local school boards and teachers have made the decisions about what students should be taught, as well as how much should be spent on public schools. This has turned out to be a mixed blessing. The good news was that decisions were made locally and not imposed. But the bad news was that the quality of education students received was often unequal within schools and between richer and poorer communities.

State policy makers have attempted to address both problems in the last fifteen years. They have sought to establish common learning standards for all students and to enforce them with new high-stakes tests. Many states are attempting to equalize the funds available for education in different communities as well. But there are disturbing trends. The first is the dramatic increase in the amount of testing going on in our nation's schools. Less often mentioned is surrendering of important decisions about what's worth learning into the hands of a very small number of "experts" and policy makers.

Often, the decisions of the "experts" and politicians run counter both to common sense and to what the majority of Americans believe is most important in education. We have already seen that many of the things employers and college professors consider most important—motivation, work habits, curiosity, and respect for others—do not appear on any state tests.

What about "regular" Americans—the people who have traditionally made the community-based decisions about what should be taught in public schools—parents, teachers, and the general public? What do they want? Let's look at an interesting national study. Then we will find out what happens when local communities have extended discussions about what is most important to know and what a high school diploma should mean.

The Public Agenda Foundation has completed the most thoughtful research on what Americans believe to be essential for all students to learn today. Quite wisely, they asked respondents to list what each group considered "absolutely essential" to be taught—requiring individuals to, in effect, create a priority list. If you do not do this, the list of all the things Americans would like to see taught quickly becomes overwhelming and unrealistic—as we've seen with the new education standards.

The table on page 47 lists, in order of importance, all subjects that at least 60 percent of parents and teachers considered essential for their local public school curriculum:[6]

While there are some differences in emphasis between groups on a few of the categories, this list shows a remarkably high degree of general agreement about things Americans consider most important to learn. What is equally interesting is the list of subjects that fewer than 60 percent of those surveyed considered absolutely essential: specific science subjects like biology, chemistry, and physics; practical job skills; advanced mathematics; the history and geography of foreign countries; specific works of classic and modern literature; and sports.

The disparity—especially between the subjects most frequently taught and now tested in American public high schools and those most Americans consider essential—is simply stunning. And then when you look at a typical

WHAT'S "ESSENTIAL" TO TEACH	PARENTS	TEACHERS	GENERAL PUBLIC
Basic reading, writing, and math skills	91%	98%	92%
Good work habits such as being responsible, on time, and disciplined	79%	92%	83%
Computer skills and media technology	78%	88%	80%
The value of hard work	77%	84%	78%
Values such as honesty and tolerance of others	71%	80%	74%
Habits of good citizenship such as voting and caring about the nation	64%	78%	66%
How to deal with social problems like drugs and family breakdown	63%	65%	64%
American history and American geography	61%	83%	63%
Curiosity and love of learning	61%	69%	57%

high school budget and realize how much is spent on the sports program relative to academics, you have to wonder: Who is making the most important decisions about the education priorities in this country and with what information?

Most Americans have a great deal of common sense—more than we give them credit for. When you ask them to really think about and set priorities for what students need to learn today for work, lifelong learning, citizenship, and personal growth and health their replies are remarkably thoughtful. But education policy makers seldom ask or listen. And the result is that many of our current public school reform policies are utterly lacking in common sense.

Can communities have thoughtful conversations about what all students should know? And if so, what happens when they do? Let me briefly relate the story of one typical American community that had such conversations.

A suburb of Hartford, Connecticut, Windsor seems outwardly to be a typical, pleasant bedroom community—the kind that has become the bedrock of America. Its school system, with about five thousand students in five elementary, two middle, and one high school, is almost a perfect statistical mirror of the national average—as were its standardized test scores. But, as is more often the case than we care to admit, beneath these appearances was a deeply divided community, with different groups competing for power and financial resources. The community, with a 45 percent minority population, was also racially divided.

Of course, these tensions and divisions were played out in local school board meetings. With the local Democratic and Republican committees choosing the slate of school board candidates, and often exchanging places as the majority from one year to the next, board meetings had degenerated into polemical political debates then often went on late into the night, and little real work was accomplished.

Dick Silverman was chosen to be superintendent of the Windsor public schools in 1997. To strengthen his schools and to increase the financial support he needed to make long overdue improvements in teaching and curriculum, Dick knew he had to first reunite his community and to involve them more directly in their schools.

One of his first steps was to meet individually with all nine school board members, as well as with each person who was running for a board position in the upcoming election. He also met one-on-one with the town's leaders from both political parties, as well as attended meetings of the various community organizations. I was brought in as a consultant to conduct confidential interviews with school board members and community leaders and to help plan a process for bringing the community together to discuss education issues.

Dick and I both found that, privately, leaders of both political parties were tired of the polarized debates that had paralyzed the community's decision making. They also understood that to attract new employers to the area and to maintain the real estate values in the community, their public school system had to be improved. Perhaps even more important, they also had a desire to re-create the sense of community that many felt had been lost in recent years.

In consultation with a newly elected school board, Dick set out to create a comprehensive process for involving the entire community in discussions about the future of education in Windsor. He invited community leaders from every kind of organization in town to serve on a steering committee—representatives from the town council and chamber of commerce, the head of the local chapter of the American Association of Retired Persons, local business leaders, representatives from both the conservative taxpayers' group and the more liberal education support organization, the chief of police, union representatives, and, of course, parents, students, teachers, and school board members. More than twenty-five people agreed to serve.

Dick and I presented a draft plan to the steering committee, which called for the sponsorship of a series of focus groups. The purpose of these in-depth discussions was to create community consensus about the goals of the Windsor public schools. The committee responded very positively to the draft plan and made excellent suggestions for ensuring that the effort was perceived to be objective. And they gave the initiative a name: Schooling for Community Success.

Over the next six months, everyone who wanted to participate in a focus group was included in one. Led by a trained moderator and note-taker, more than six hundred people in the community—as well as teachers and high school students—met in small groups to discuss the same four questions:

- What are the most important things for Windsor's graduates to know and be able to do?
- How will we know if students have mastered the expected competencies?
- What are the immediate priorities for educational improvement in Windsor?
- What are the roles and responsibilities of schools, parents, businesses, and the community in contributing to what students need to know and be able to do?

All of the answers were recorded and made publicly available to anyone interested. Copies of what came to be nicknamed "the yellow pages"—for their size and yellow cover—were put in each school and in the town library. Meanwhile, a small subgroup of the steering committee set to work plowing through the data.

To the surprise of many, the responses to the focus group questions were remarkably consistent and showed a great deal of agreement around a few basic education goals. The goals listed below were then presented to the school board, who approved them unanimously:

Goal I: All Windsor Public School students will acquire and demonstrate core knowledge and essential skills that emphasize understanding, application, and communication.

Goal II: All Windsor Public School students will demonstrate thinking and reasoning skills.

Goal III: All Windsor Public School students will demonstrate motivation and persistence to learn.

Goal IV: All Windsor Public School students will understand, respect, and act in accordance with universal values.

Goal V: All Windsor Public School students will demonstrate readiness for adult roles.

Developed along with each goal was a one-paragraph rationale that explained what the goal meant and why it was important. The committee also generated a list of expectations for each goal that began to spell out more concretely what students were expected to be able to know and do and how they were expected to act.

Once ratified by the school board, the goals became the basis for all decisions in the schools about both educational and financial priorities. They also provided a framework for talking about a continuous improvement process—what kinds of school and district changes would be needed in order to accomplish the goals.

Besides becoming more clear about what the community expected of its students, something else important was accomplished as well. The town began to experience itself as a community once again. There has been a dramatic increase in the levels of parental and community involvement in all of the schools. More adults are spending more time in classrooms. School and town government leaders have forged much closer working relationships. And people in and out of the schools have begun to feel freer to talk about long-taboo issues, like the racial divisions in the community and what might be done to overcome them—both for students and adults. School board meetings took on a very different tone as well. There was respectful dialogue, work got done, and meetings ended much earlier than before.

The crucial test came in the spring after this process was completed when the board had to vote on the next year's education budget. Dick had proposed a substantial increase in school funding. When the final vote to adopt the budget was taken, it was unanimous for the first time since anyone could remember.

The Windsor story is not unique. I have helped a dozen or more communities all over the country create consensus about what they want students to know and be able to do—from districts in rural New Hampshire and Wisconsin, the hollers of West Virginia, and the suburbs of Cincinnati to groups of schools in Las Cruces, New Mexico, Boston, Chicago, and Milwaukee.

In every community, a number of the results are quite similar. First, community members want to be involved and are grateful to leaders who create the opportunity for meaningful dialogue. Public trust for educators is greatly strengthened. With greater trust, public support for public education also flourishes. Local funding for public education increases substantially, as does the number of people offering to volunteer in the schools. Education is no longer seen as a partisan issue, but as everyone's responsibility.

A second finding from my experience with this process is that communities have very little difficulty in coming to agreement about what's most important to learn. In all of the communities where I have facilitated discussions, the list of local education priorities ends up being very similar to what the Public Agenda Foundation found to be important in their national study.

The results are not always the same, however, and what differences that do exist from one community to the next are significant. For example, the two rural communities where I have helped organize discussions about what students should know both identified entrepreneurship as a vital skill they wanted their students to master. The reasons were fundamental: if more of the younger generation did not learn how to run successful businesses, there would be no jobs for them, and they would have to leave the community to earn a living. Such differences illustrate the importance of local groups—rather than state panels of experts—making the decision of what they want their children to learn.

WHAT ABOUT VALUES?

Another reason why local communities, rather than the state, must decide what is most important to learn is the issue of values. Look, again, at the list of what the Public Agenda Foundation found to be on the "essential to learn" list for parents, teachers, and citizens: values. Teaching universal values is one of Windsor's goals as well.

In years of doing this work, I have found that virtually every community believes that parents are the first and best teachers of values but that basic values should also be reinforced by schools. How can this be, you wonder, when it seems that nearly every day one reads about some bitter school debate around the teaching of values? It is my view that both conservatives and liberals have greatly confused and polarized the issues around the teaching of values.

To get clarity, we need to separate the issue of values from religion. The American system of government is predicated on a separation of church and state, but democracy is not a value-free form of governance. We are committed to each person having a voice and to equality of opportunity for all. In practice, this means that communities and individuals from diverse backgrounds must practice tolerance, listen to one another, and compromise in order for our system of government to function. As we learned in the last chapter, these same values are now important in the workplace as well, because of the increasing emphasis on teamwork.

Most Americans intuitively understand the importance of certain values for citizenship and work and believe that schools have a role to play in strengthening our capacities as citizens to govern and live in an increasingly diverse society. As we've seen, a Public Agenda Foundation study found that 71 percent of all Americans believe that it is more important to teach values than academic subjects in our public schools.[7] When Public Agenda researchers probed which specific values should be taught, they found "overwhelming majorities of Americans—across geographic and demographic lines" agreed on certain core values: 95 percent of all Americans believe honesty and respect for others "regardless of their racial or ethnic background" should be taught. And 93 percent said, "Schools should teach students to solve problems without violence." Other values near the top of the list of what Americans believe should be taught in schools all underscored a concern for equality, fairness, and "getting along."

The authors of the Public Agenda study conclude:

> The findings . . . suggest among the general public a longing for harmony and civility and some desire to put discord in the past. The public school system has played a historic role in enabling diverse Americans to learn about each other, and live together without bloodshed—a goal that many other nations have not been able to achieve. During the 1950s and 1960s, the public schools became the symbol of the nation's moral judgment that African-Americans and white Americans should live together in equality.
>
> Few would argue that the United States has lived up to all of its goals, and it is indisputable that prejudice, anger, misunderstanding, and distrust continue to divide the country along racial and ethnic lines. Regardless of these failures, the vast majority of Americans accept the goal, and they want the public schools to play a central role in passing that goal along to their children.

Values in Everyday Life: Two School Stories

In addition to separating the issue of values from religion, we need to dispel two widely held myths about the issue of values in schools. The first is that values are only a problem for schools that serve poor kids, and the second is that lack of values is only a problem for students. To make these points more clear, let me briefly relate the true stories of two schools that have struggled with the issue of values.

The first is the story of an elite independent boarding school in New England. This school, which I shall call St. Joan, is highly competitive and academically rigorous. It sends a large percentage of its graduates on to leading universities and so is frequently held up as a model of outstanding secondary education.

But this is a school where the students had taken over, and when I visited several years ago, adults were still struggling to regain control. In one year, students set fire to the outdoor Christmas tree of the head of the school. And when spring came, the school head discovered that an antique dresser from his house had been found floating in the river, miles from the school. Meanwhile back in the dorms, drugs and alcohol were widely available on a nightly basis.

So the trustees installed new leadership. But the struggle to reassert some standards of decency continued. One Saturday night, the student improvisational drama group gave a performance for most of the school. The featured act was an explicitly sexual and extremely vulgar skit that ridiculed the eighteen-year-old daughter of the head of the school. Teachers in the audience did nothing to stop the performance. When the associate head of the school announced the suspension of the students involved during a schoolwide chapel the next week, three-quarters of the student body walked out.

I talked with the associate head of the school several months later, and she was still somewhat in shock. A woman who had recently come to this position after many years of experience in public schools, she could not believe that students from "good families" could behave so badly. She was also stunned at the adult behavior. Her biggest struggle was in trying to get the teachers to admit there was a serious problem with student behavior and values and to take concerted action as adults. They preferred to "look the other way" rather than to get involved.

While somewhat extreme, this case is not atypical. In his book *Privileged Ones*, Robert Coles describes the "sense of entitlement" that characterizes the behavior of many students from upper-middle-class families.[8] And in my first book, I related the story of how adults at the Brimmer and May School, concerned about the problem of lack of respect, created a series of schoolwide conversations. Students and adults worked together to identify the problems and to create a much stronger sense of a caring community.

I also worked for a year with one of the most highly ranked public high schools in the country and discovered that struggles around values and behaviors in elite public schools are somewhat different but equally serious. Academically, the school was indeed a challenging and rigorous environment and highly successful in terms of getting students into the most selective colleges. Despite this, I discovered through some focus group work that it was a place where many students and adults were unhappy.

The students complained about going to a "segregated" school. There were four academic tracks, and students from these tracks ate lunch in four different parts of the school and almost never socialized together. They related to each other largely in terms of racial and religious stereotypes.

One young woman summarized the concerns of many of the students when she said, "I'm going to graduate in a few months and go into a world where I will have to get along with different kinds of people. And I won't know the first thing about how to do it. All we ever do here is go to classes and hang out with kids like ourselves."

Parents were concerned about the competitive stresses in kids' lives. They wanted their children to go to "good colleges," of course, but a number feared that students would think getting into a "name brand" school was all there was to life—and to school. Some worried about what happens to curiosity and love of learning for its own sake in the process.

The support staff—school security guards, teaching assistants, cafeteria workers, and so on—felt that they were being treated as servants by some of the students. They were also upset about how the students left trash everywhere in the building and thought teachers needed to pay more attention to student behavior.

But many of the teachers, it turned out, were more preoccupied with how they treated one another. Apparently, there was a kind of "cold war" being fought between older and younger teachers over issues of educational philosophy. The older teachers tended to value more academic content and expertise, while many of the younger teaches felt "process skills"— problem solving and teamwork—were more important in the classroom. Some teachers were also concerned about how some older teachers spoke to students with sarcasm. Each felt the other group did not respect them and their ideas.

To this faculty's great credit, they were able to acknowledge these problems and make a commitment to change the climate of the school. When I presented the data I had gathered in a faculty meeting and talked briefly about the importance of a good education including standards for the heart or emotional intelligence, no one questioned my findings. They wanted to talk about what could be done.

I worked with the school for the next year to create a series of small-group faculty conversations aimed at developing a deeper understanding of the issues and possible solutions. Just the fact that faculty had named the problem of lack of respect among themselves and had begun to discuss the issues together in a civil manner helped to improve the climate of the school.

However, a number of the faculty leaders came to believe that the very structure of the school was at the heart of the problem. Neither teachers nor students really knew one another; nor could they know one another in such a large, impersonal institutional environment. When I last visited the school, they had begun to discuss creating a very different structure for the school—breaking it down into smaller, more autonomous houses—in order to promote a greater sense of community among students and teamwork with the faculty.

Whatever this school may ultimately decide about a new structure, many adults in the building have come to understand the importance of dealing with values in the school and that you couldn't simply lecture about values as if it were just another academic subject. Real lessons about values begin with creating opportunities for conversations about behaviors that are of concern—both adult and student—behaviors that we want to promote, and the choices we all face daily.

NEW STRUCTURES FOR DECISION MAKING

Obviously, the decision to teach values and the naming of specific values is not something that can or should be done at the state level. Nor is it simply a matter of holding a school board hearing on the subject—as they are too often dominated by a vocal few who represent fringe elements in the community, rather than the mainstream. In the story above, face-to-face conversations were central to the process of coming to agreement about the importance of values. How can this be done on a community-wide basis?

In my experience, the only way that communities can come to consensus on these issues is through the same focus group process that I described in the Windsor School District story. Public opinion research expert Daniel Yankelovich describes the difference between polls that measure "mass opinion," which is "top of the head" and likely to change, versus "public judgment," which is the result of "working through" complex issues and is far more likely to endure over time.[9] The teaching of values and decisions about the things that are most important to learn require conversations that allow citizens time to "work through" complex issues and reflect and learn together.

This process has another important benefit as well. It begins to change the behavior of adults. I've seen it over and over. Even in places where factions had been at war with one another for years, a new spirit is born out of the shared conversations. The ground rules we use for the focus groups are part of the answer. They encourage dialogue rather than debate. As we go around the circle, everyone has a chance to be heard, and no one can dominate. We agree to disagree, without being disagreeable.

The focus group process thus asks people to practice the habit of civility. Along the way, many seem to rediscover the value of thoughtful conversation about important issues—a process Yankelovich calls "dialogic learning."[10] Individuals and groups come together to solve an education problem for the young, and they create community for themselves as adults. With a greater sense of shared civic-mindedness and civility, some adults begin to see that they have important roles to play in schools, beyond merely paying taxes or agreeing on education goals. Once again, the course of events in Windsor is an interesting case study.

More than a year after initiating the focus group process, the steering committee has resumed meeting. They're talking about what other responsibilities, besides setting goals, citizens might have for supporting public education.

A number are asking how students' mastery of the newly minted goals might best be assessed. They know that the state-mandated standardized test is not the answer, so they are considering a number of ways in which students might do projects where they can demonstrate mastery of complex skills. It is what I call the "merit badge" approach to learning and assessment and is a topic we will consider in the next chapter.

As the Windsor steering committee thinks about issues of assessment, they have a new consideration in mind. They want the community to be involved in helping to judge students' work. And they're hoping to find more ways for students to learn in the community as well.

I met with them soon after the Columbine High School tragedy. Several thought it wasn't impossible for something like that to occur in Windsor's own high school. And they knew why. Too many children are growing up without much of an adult presence in their lives. It wasn't just the parents' fault. Some steering committee members were beginning to realize the roles and responsibilities all adults—not just parents—have in helping to mentor the young.

Police Chief Kevin Searles saw the problem most clearly. "I walk down the halls of the high school, and the kids standing against the wall who don't know me kind of stare with a hostile attitude. But the students whose names I know—even if they've been in trouble—have a completely different response. They smile and say hi. They know I know who they are and that I'm concerned for them. Every student needs that," Kevin said quietly. "Every student needs to be known by adults and to be more a part of the community."

TOWARD THE "NEW VILLAGE SCHOOL"

A small number of academics, politicians, and psychometricians are making the critical decisions about what all students should know in America today. And their decisions are too often influenced by a combination of outdated thinking, narrow academic interests, and political and financial considerations that have little to do with what's most important for students to know and be able to do in the twenty-first century. Rarely is the debate about standards and curriculum informed by an inquiry into the competencies most needed by students in a rapidly changing world.

Paraphrasing French statesman Georges Clemenceau, who said, "War is too important to leave to the generals," what students should know is too important a decision to be left to the "experts" and the politicians.

I believe that American citizens can and must decide what's most important to learn as well as the values the community believes should be reinforced by schools. Indeed, many groups are successfully doing this work in schools and communities today. And they are realizing that one of the greatest benefits for communities who come together to make such decisions is the return to civil discourse, volunteerism, and other behaviors that build community. In my talks around the country, I find that a majority of educators, parents, and citizens understand and support this ideal of rebuilding community around local schools by creating what I call "New Village Schools." To create an effective school improvement strategy based on this vision, we must explore some new answers to difficult questions.

Many of the questions come under the headings of accountability and scale. For example, how do we assess things like "problem-solving skills?" And who should do the assessments? How do we hold local communities accountable for education results? Indeed, what constitutes a "local" community? And how can this strategy be applied in large cities? Finally, if local communities have greater control over their educational goals, what, then, are the roles for the state and federal governments?

We consider these questions in the next chapter.

3

HOW DO WE HOLD STUDENTS
AND SCHOOLS ACCOUNTABLE?

TEN years ago, it would have been difficult to imagine creating a system of public education based on the New Village School idea. One reason is that there were too few examples of new kinds of small public schools to generalize about larger possibilities. This is no longer true. Today, as we will see, there are thousands of new small public schools around the country that bear witness to the ability of thoughtful adults to rethink what all students should know and to create dramatically more effective schools.

But perhaps the greatest obstacle to creating New Village Schools has been the inability to "prove" that all students were learning and to hold schools accountable. In a world where much more is expected of students and schools, new approaches to education have to demonstrate that they can get better results. And if educators who create these schools do not believe the standardized tests in use today assess what they are teaching, then they must create new approaches to assessing students' skills.

Fortunately—for students and for education—a small group of "educational entrepreneurs" have been doing some very important "research and development" in the last fifteen years. They are creating new approaches to student assessment and school accountability, which allow us to imagine designing a system of public education where there is much greater choice of schools and curriculum, more local autonomy, and *more* accountability.

The story of this educational research and development is rich and complex—and one that has many heroes and heroines—but it lies beyond the boundaries of this book. However, the story of one school—Central Park East Secondary School—and of its founder, Deborah Meier, and first "critical friend," Ted Sizer—is important at many levels.

In some ways, the founders of Central Park East created the prototype for what I call the New Village School and a new kind of American secondary school. Their model has many innovative design concepts and incorporates a radically different approach to student and school accountability, which we shall explore more thoroughly in the next chapter. The example of Central Park East and the work of the Coalition of Essential Schools has profoundly influenced a generation of educational entrepreneurs, of which I am one.

My visit to the school in 1989 forever changed my thinking about what a good high school can and should look like.

THE CENTRAL PARK EAST STORY

The story of Central Park East Secondary School begins in 1974 in New York City's Community School District 4, located in Harlem.[1] The superintendent at that time, Anthony Alvarado, believed that a promising strategy for improving urban schools was to give parents a greater choice of the public school that their children could attend. Deborah Meier was one of the individuals Tony approached to start a new elementary school. Her school, Central Park East Elementary, was so popular that she eventually opened two sister schools.

The sixth-grade graduates of these schools ended up doing significantly better in high school than students from other elementary schools did, but Deborah was still concerned about the damaging effects on her graduates of the typical American comprehensive high school. So when Ted Sizer, a nationally recognized critic of high schools and founder of a reform group The Coalition of Essential Schools, suggested that Deborah start a high school of her own, she agreed.

Deborah's new school, and several of the other fledgling Coalition schools, were founded on a radical premise: there would be no "tracking" (grouping of students by perceived ability) at Central Park East, and all students would have the same intellectually rigorous curriculum, which would emphasize what Deborah and her teachers called "habits of mind." They defined habits of mind as a set of intellectual predispositions and skills such as the ability to observe closely and carefully; being skeptical, open-minded, and respectful of evidence; the capacity for understanding how others think and feel; and knowing how to communicate effectively in a variety of media and take a stand.[2]

Now lots of schools have high-sounding goals or mission statements that aspire to cultivate intellectual rigor, citizenship, and so on. But almost never is there any effort to find out whether students have actually acquired any of these attributes. At Central Park East, Deborah and her colleagues set out to create a set of graduation requirements and a rigorous assessment system that would enable them to determine whether students had, indeed, mastered real intellectual skills.

The Breakthrough: Graduation by "Exhibitions of Mastery"

In order to graduate from Central Park East Secondary School, students would have to earn a diploma by "exhibiting mastery" rather than serving "seat time." In virtually every high school that existed then—and in all but a handful of high schools today—students graduate when they have earned sufficient Carnegie units or credits. Students accrue credits by taking so many hours of English, social studies, science, math, and so on. The number and kinds of credits required may vary in different schools or districts, but the system is essentially the same everywhere—and is virtually unchanged since its inception in 1906.

Deborah, Ted, and other Coalition founders believed that this system of merely earning credits by spending the requisite number of hours in a class resulted in a lack of intellectual rigor. In too many high schools—especially those serving disadvantaged youth—students received a passing grade in a course by just coming to class every day. In practice, millions of students were graduating from high school with minimal skills.

Deborah proposed replacing this credit system of graduation requirements with an entirely new, "performance-based" system, or what I call a "merit badge" approach to graduation. Students could only graduate when they had earned the necessary merit badges—which were exhibitions of mastery in different intellectual and social domains. Serving seat time wasn't good enough. In fact, Deborah's system explicitly allowed for students to complete their merit badges on their own timeline. Students enter what the school calls the "Senior Institute" at eleventh grade and begin to work on their graduation requirements. Some students complete their merit badges, which the school calls "portfolio requirements," much more quickly than others and so graduate from high school sooner.

While this idea of exhibitions of mastery was, and still is, new as a concept for high school, it is hardly a new idea in education. More than two thousand years ago, the Greeks used Socratic dialogues to both develop and test students' thinking. Since the Middle Ages, students doing advanced academic work have had to appear before a panel of scholars to be examined and to explain or defend their theses. It is still the preferred form of examination in the world's elite universities. And many of the most elite private high schools require students to do some form of senior paper, speech, or project in order to graduate.

But in a public school where the enrollment was 90 percent minority youth from economically impoverished homes? It was a daring proposition. And then when you look at what the requirements are, the idea seems almost foolish. In order to earn a diploma at Central Park East Secondary School, students were (and still are) required to exhibit mastery in a total of fourteen different areas. Students document their work in what the school calls "portfolios."

Graduation Portfolio Requirements at CPESS

What follows is a description of the portfolio elements in each of the fourteen categories of competency required for graduation at Central Park East.[3]

1. *Postgraduate Plan*: Each student must outline his or her current purpose for earning a diploma. As the *Senior Institute Handbook* (CPESS, 1990) notes, "Reflecting on purposes helps to set goals." Long- and short-range career and life goals, financial concerns, living arrangements, and indicators of progress, such as examinations, interviews, and letters of reference, must be included in this section. The Postgraduate Plan is begun at entry to the Senior Institute and provides direction for all the student's subsequent work in the Senior Institute. It is revised as needed and revisited for evaluation at the time of graduation.

2. *Autobiography*: This gives the student another opportunity to reflect on his or her life and to plan for the future. A project of the student's choosing is required. It may examine family history, special events, relationships, values, or beliefs in any of a variety of media—written or oral narrative, essay, art, video, drama, music, or other form selected by the student.

3. *School/Community Service and Internship*: Opportunities for working and serving others are part of student experiences each year starting in seventh grade. Students must develop a formal resume of their past work and employment experiences along with a project that demonstrates what they have learned from one or more of these experiences. Projects can include essays, videos, work samples, reference letters, or other demonstrations of their accomplishments combined with evidence of what they have learned.

4. *Ethics and Social Issues*: Students can demonstrate their capacity to see multiple perspectives, weigh and use evidence, and reason about social and moral issues in any number of ways—by staging a debate, writing an editorial, discussing important issues raised in a novel or film, or creating another project that demonstrates these capacities.

5. *Fine Arts and Aesthetics*: Creative expression and creative appreciation are both evaluated. Students must create a "hands-on" exhibition of performance in any of the arts and must offer evidence of knowledge or understanding in an aesthetic area by studying or critiquing a work, an artist, or a field of artistic expression.

6. *Mass Media*: Students must show that they understand how different forms of media work and how they affect people and their thinking, including the CPESS Habits of Mind. This understanding can be demonstrated through many types of projects or activities, ranging from essays to exhibits or media presentations, and must include a relevant bibliography.

7. *Practical Skills*: In keeping with CPESS's commitment to preparing students for all aspects of life, they must show evidence of working knowledge in a number of areas—ranging from health and medical care to employment, citizenship, independent living, computers and technology, and legal rights—in a variety of ways, ranging from securing a driver's license to registering to vote to demonstrating the ability to operate a computer.

8. *Geography*: A teacher-made test and a student-designed performance assessment are used to evaluate geographical knowledge and the ability to use geographical tools such as maps and globes.

9. *Second Language and/or Dual Language*: All students must demonstrate competence to work in a language other than English as a speaker, listener, reader, and writer. (This requirement may be met through the New York State language proficiency exam or a College Board examination.) In addition, all students must describe their personal experience with dual language issues and be prepared to discuss a key social or cultural issue associated with language use.

10. *Science and Technology*: Students must demonstrate knowledge in traditional ways—a summary of the work they have completed in high school and passage of a teacher—made or state competency test—as well as in performances that demonstrate use of scientific methodology (e.g., conducting and documenting an experiment) and awareness of how science is used in the modern world (e.g., by staging a debate or conducting research on a scientific development analyzing social costs and benefits).

11. *Mathematics*: Students must demonstrate basic skills knowledge by passing a state competency test and a teacher-made test. In addition they must demonstrate higher-order thinking abilities by developing a project using mathematics for political, civic, or consumer purposes (e.g., social science statistics or polling, evaluation data, architectural blueprints) and either scientific or pure mathematics (e.g., using mathematics in a scientific application and/or studying a mathematical topic or problem for its own sake).

12. *Literature*: Students prepare a list of texts they have read in a variety of genres to serve as the basis for discussion with the graduation committee. They also submit samples of their own essays about literary works or figures, demonstrating their capacity to reflect on and communicate effectively about literary products and ideas.

13. *History*: In addition to passing a state competency test or faculty-designed test in history, students must prepare an overview of the areas of history they have studied in secondary school and a timeline of major events and persons. They must also demonstrate an understanding of historical work by conducting historical research using primary and secondary sources and developing a bibliography. They apply the Habits of Mind by drawing connections between and among past and present events, weighing and using evidence, speculating on other possibilities, and evaluating how history is used or abused in current debates.

14. *Physical Challenge*: Students demonstrate and/or document their participation and proficiency in any team or individual competitive or non-competitive sport or activity over the past four years. The goal is to encourage the development of lifelong health habits and attitudes of independence, interdependence, personal responsibility, and sportsmanship.

In addition to completing all fourteen elements of the portfolio, seven of the portfolio elements had to be presented—explained and defended—to a graduation committee that consisted of the student's faculty advisor, another faculty member, a third adult of the student's choosing, and another student. Four of the seven elements presented to the committee had to be in the core subject areas: science and technology, mathematics, literature, and history. The remainder could be of the student's choosing.

A PERFORMANCE-BASED K–12 CURRICULUM

Central Park East Secondary School is an exciting example of how one school can break the mold and create an approach to education that is both more meaningful for students and more accountable for results. But the school must deal with widely varying levels of skills of its incoming seventh-graders. It also must operate within the constraints and conventions of the city and state educational bureaucracy. As I write this book, the battle is still being fought over whether Central Park East and its thirty-eight sister high schools in the New York Performance Standards Consortium will have to require that students take the mandatory state regents exams, in addition to all the school's requirements, in order to receive a high school diploma. (This is a problem to which we will return later in this chapter.)

And so the question remains: What would a performance-based or merit badge education system look like if it were created from scratch and was consistent throughout a student's school experience? What if it were "the system," instead of being a challenge and a perceived threat to an existing system?

Five thousand miles from New York City, a tiny district in rural Alaska called Chugach is pushing the envelope of student and teacher accountability and assessment with some extraordinary results. I recently had an opportunity to visit three of their schools and talk at length with students, teachers, parents, and Superintendent Rich DeLorenzo, the moving force behind the creation of a truly performance-based education system.

The Chugach School District was created twenty years ago and serves mostly native villages in very remote locations—almost all of which are accessible only by plane or boat. When Rich became assistant superintendent seven years ago, the district had some of the worst California Achievement Test (CAT) scores in the state, and only one of the district's graduates had ever gone on to college.

As the district analyzed the problem, they came to see that most students and their parents had no idea what kinds of skills were required to be successful in the adult world, beyond the realm of village life. Few knew what skills were needed to apply for a job in a city or to a college—let alone succeed in either. And the traditional academic curriculum gave them no help in deciphering this foreign world.

The district's first step was to involve all the villagers in something called Alaska Onward Towards Excellence. It is a process of leading communities through discussions of what skills are needed to be a successful adult and what the schools' priorities should be—and is very similar to the methodology I've used in a number of communities. The villagers' list of expectations was then compared with a list developed by business and community leaders "on the outside" in Anchorage. Much to the villagers' surprise, there was substantial consensus on the most important competencies for success in adult life. More surprising still was the commitment of the school district to create an entirely new curriculum and assessment system aimed at ensuring that students mastered the most important skill areas.

The system has gone through a number of revisions and continues to be improved every year. But the fundamental concept remains the same. Students must demonstrate proficiency through multiple forms of assessment in ten areas of standards:

1. Mathematics
2. Reading
3. Technology
4. Social sciences
5. Writing
6. Personal/social/health
7. Career development
8. Cultural awareness and expression
9. Service learning
10. Science

Each standard area is then broken down into between seven and twelve different levels of mastery. Think of them as the equivalent of Cub Scout, Boy Scout, and Eagle Scout levels of proficiency—with additional levels added. The minimum level required to receive a diploma is defined in every one of the ten standard areas, *and students do not graduate until they have met the minimum requirement for each standard.* In fact, the state has granted the district a waver that permits them to completely bypass the regular system of credits in favor of this performance-based approach.

At a very early age, every student and his or her parents know exactly what must be accomplished to receive a diploma—and why. Students set out to work their way through the different levels of proficiency required in each content area. Each student creates an individual learning plan (ILP) every academic quarter, with assistance from the teacher. In a given quarter, a student may decide to work primarily on the writing proficiency, for example, and the student and teacher will agree on what kinds of projects will help a student reach the next level of mastery.

Parents review and sign their children's ILPs each quarter and talk with the teacher about how they can support their child's learning goals. Taped to each student's desk is a one-page summary chart that lists the ten standards down the page and the levels of mastery across the top of the page. The teachers mark off exactly at what level each student has progressed to in every skill area, so that a student has a kind of bar graph snapshot of his or her academic progress.

At each level and in all ten competency areas, students must show mastery of specific skills and/or content, analytic capacity, and the ability to apply knowledge. The content for academic subjects is aligned with the Alaska state standards or to the standards of a national professional organization, but Chugach is selective, rather than encyclopedic, in what content students are expected to master. A detailed district evaluation form summarizes the content, analytic, and applied learning requirements at every level in each skill area. The required level for graduation in science (Level VI) is illustrative:[4]

Content Knowledge

Students must study and master a minimum of two (2) of the following content areas for level V and then a minimum of two (2) others from this list for level VI:

1. Structure of atoms
2. Structure and properties of matter
3. Chemical reactions
4. Motions and forces
5. Conservation of energy and increase in disorder
6. Interaction of energy and matter
7. The cell
8. Molecular basis of heredity
9. Biological evolution
10. Interdependence of organisms
11. Matter, energy, and organization in living systems
12. Behavior of organisms
13. Energy in the earth system
14. Geochemical cycles
15. Origin and evolution of the earth system
16. Origin and evolution of the universe

Notice that students can make some choices about the academic content of greatest interest to them. Notice also that the academic content is not divided by the traditional boundaries called biology, chemistry, physics, earth science, and so on. It is integrated around important concepts.

The list of competencies students must master in Level VI science in order to graduate is even more impressive. Here students have no choice— as mastery of skills is considered more important than memorization of particular content. Again, I quote from the Chugach School District Report Card:

Developing Questions: Is able to convert a question into a hypothesis and a hypothesis to a question; explains what types of questions science cannot answer.

Designing Investigations: Designs investigations that control all but one variable; designs inquiries that result in an accurate explanation or model.

Conducting Investigations: Works in a systematic manner; keeps neat, accurate notes while conducting self-designed investigations.

Communicating Results: Defends explanation/model orally and in writing; revises explanations based on reasoning, scientific knowledge, and evidence; evaluates and adopts alternative explanations when warranted.

In practice, students begin working on some of these skills at a very young age. In one of the villages I visited, two eleven-year-old students explained to me how they had developed a hypothesis about what would happen to bugs in a puddle when it got cold. They then observed the puddle as it froze over for the first time in the season and recorded their observations and conclusions.

The list of expectations is as demanding in all of the other academic content areas. And in all ten skill areas, the district has developed expectations, curricula, and assessments that go beyond merely what must be mastered in order to receive a diploma so that a student can progress and show advanced mastery in areas of particular skill or interest.

Equally impressive, the Chugach team has developed a set of competency requirements and a curriculum to teach them in the realm of what Murnane and Levy called soft skills. Students must show proficiency in the skill area the district calls Personal/Social/Health, for example, and the list of requirements in this category is as challenging as any that can be found in the more traditional academic domains. Here is a description of the graduation requirements (Level VII) in this skill area:

Personal

- Demonstrates ability to find community resources or continuing education resources (health clinics, city/tribal councils, employment services, trade school, college, etc.)
- Displays appropriate positive behavior in a variety of situations.
- Evaluates responsibility and consequences of one's choices and actions.

Social

- Applies transferable personal/social skills and appropriate, positive behavior in a variety of situations (uses tact, employs negotiating and leadership skills).
- Employs strategies for dealing with peer pressure.
- Employs techniques to foster positive personal relationships in a group setting.
- Applies skills for creating and maintaining healthy social and professional relationships.

Health
- Analyzes personal and social changes and responsibilities associated with pregnancy and birth (including prevention of birth defects and effective family planning options).
- Demonstrates all skills required for obtaining first aid certification.
- Creates a personal health plan to maintain proper nutrition and exercise.

Many of these skills are taught and assessed through the district's unique "applied learning" curriculum, where students spend a week or two every year in a place called Anchorage House, where they live and learn with students from many other districts. Here the curriculum is very practical. In the first visit students learn how to take buses and how to conduct phone interviews to get needed information from strangers, for example.

Older students' Anchorage House curriculum becomes progressively more demanding. At advanced levels, they are required, first, to spend time observing adults in different job settings as a way of exploring potential careers, and then to complete a successful work internship. They must also make a budget for their week, shop for and prepare all their own meals, and govern themselves as a group.

In my visits to the three Chugach schools, I had a firsthand opportunity to assess the impact of this revolutionary education system on both students and parents. A high degree of trust and respect between the villagers and the teachers has developed as the district delivered on its promise of creating a curriculum based on what adults in the village (and elsewhere) had agreed were the prerequisites of adult success. Parents also said that, for the first time, they really knew their children's academic strengths and weaknesses and how they could help them improve.

But it is the students' motivations for learning that have been the most profoundly impacted. An eleventh-grade young woman explained, "Under the old system, I was just supposed to study a bunch of stuff. It was boring, and I didn't know why I had to learn it. Now I know exactly what I have to do to graduate and to get a job or go to college."

While many of the skills they learned were practical, all of the students whom I interviewed said they planned to go to college.

NEW APPROACHES TO SCHOOL ACCOUNTABILITY

The system of student assessment at both Central Park East and in the Chugach School District creates a high degree of internal school accountability and consistency of standards for students. Student work is on display for all to see. In both places, adults have to discuss and agree on what constitutes a pass or a mark of distinction for each portfolio and exhibition, and peers review one another's work. But how do the adults know if they have set the standards high enough? How can a school be held accountable?

Most people still believe that the best answer is standardized test scores. In fact, some schools that have developed performance-based systems have also done very well on traditional standardized tests. In Chugach, for example, the district average scores on the CAT (a nationally used standardized test) went from 28 percent to 71 percent in reading and from 36 percent to 79 percent in math in only five years.

But there are several problems with using only standardized tests to determine whether a school or a district is providing students with an appropriately challenging or rigorous education. First, most standardized tests in use today do not begin to assess the sophisticated competencies that Central Park East and other schools expect students to master. And second, many very good students are not necessarily good test-takers. The ability to answer large numbers of arbitrary or even ridiculous-sounding questions in a very short period of time is not a skill many students master.

Then there is the problem of race. Although they may be extremely able when judged by other measures, students from poor and minority backgrounds generally do not score as well on standardized tests as Caucasian and Asian students do. No one is sure why, but the fact poses a significant dilemma for schools serving these populations. How can they determine if their students are being well educated?

Deborah Meier and her colleagues took the problem of school accountability very seriously—as do the leaders in Chugach. First, in both places they collect data on a range of other measures of a school's success—notably the student dropout and college attendance rates. In Chugach, you'll recall that not a single student had completed college under the old system. In last year's graduating class—the first to complete the new curriculum—80 percent of the students went on to enroll in college, while the remaining 20 percent entered business.

Central Park East has been operating for a longer period of time in a system whose numbers are all too well known, and so they have much more comparative data to judge their results. The dropout rate in New York City's comprehensive high schools is about 50 percent. Out of every one hundred ninth graders, only fifty or so end up with a diploma four years later. In fact, the numbers are much worse in high schools that serve predominantly minority populations, as Central Park East does. Citywide, less than half of the graduating class ends up going on to college.

In the early 1990s, Central Park East Secondary School had virtually the same numbers of special education students and students who were recipients of a free or reduced fee lunch (a widely used indicator of poverty) as other New York high schools. But in its first three years, Central Park East graduated more than 95 percent of its students. And 90 percent of its first three graduating classes went on to college—most (80 percent) to four-year institutions—according to David Bensman's follow-up studies of Central Park East Secondary School graduates.[5] Most of these students were the first in his or her family to attend college.

Not only did students get into college, but they also stayed in and did well. Once again, Bensman's interviews with and data for CPESS graduates document remarkable results. Students reported being well prepared for college, and their rates of academic persistence were substantially higher than national averages—despite often feeling socially isolated and struggling with severe financial pressures.

But this wasn't enough for Meier and her colleagues. She decided to create an "auditing" system as a way to assess the quality of students' work. Every year, she invited outsiders—professors from college, leaders from corporations, and peers from other public and private high schools—to sit down with teachers and review student portfolios selected at random. She asked them to consider whether the student work met *their* criteria for competence in different skill and subject content areas, according to what is required for both college and adult work. This idea of using outsiders to help evaluate student work on an ongoing basis is one that many schools have adopted and adapted.

THE SCHOOL QUALITY REVIEW CONCEPT

Inviting outsiders to assess student work and even school quality is not a new idea. Regional secondary school associations have used periodic visits by teams of educators from other schools as a part of a process of acquiring and maintaining accreditation. Other countries—notably England—have used teams of examiners to assess the quality of public schools for several decades. Recognizing the limits of information that standardized testing can provide about school quality, networks of new public schools and even some states have begun to experiment with using outside teams of evaluators to conduct school quality reviews. In many respects, these reviews, if done properly, can give far more reliable and in-depth information about the strengths and weakness of schools than can the school's profile of standardized test results.

School Quality Review programs vary according to the sponsoring organization or state, but they frequently share three common elements. First are agreed-upon *standards for effective schools*, which have been collaboratively developed by representatives from groups of schools, professional associations, and/or state agencies. Second, is a series of topics or questions, which school communities consider periodically as a reference for *self-study*. Third are *periodic visits by teams of external reviewers* who use the school standards and results of the school's own self-study to assess the overall work of the school. The result of the visit is usually a written, public report that describes commendations and recommendations for the visited school's consideration.

The model of the School Quality Review process developed by the New York State Department of Education in 1992, under the visionary leadership of State Commissioner Thomas Sobel, is an excellent example of the process. It was adapted from the British system of school assessment and is well documented by Jacqueline Ancess in her publication *Outside/Inside, Inside/Outside: Developing and Implementing the School Quality Review*.[6]

The standards for a good school are, in the New York example, captured in a document called "Values and Assumptions." The kinds of questions and data School Quality Review teams will look at in their school visits are outlined in the New York document called "Points of Departure."

Once schools have competed their own self-studies, based on the two documents mentioned above, they are ready to host a visit by a School Quality Review Team, typically consisting of experienced educators, parents, and community and business partners. Teams would spend three or four days visiting a school, observing classes and meetings; interviewing teachers, students, administrators, parents, school staff, and community members; and reviewing test score and other data, as well as samples of student work. Once the visit was completed, the team prepares an oral report, which is presented to the school community with opportunities for questions and discussion, and a written report. The reports typically describe the activities of the visiting committee, school strengths, and areas of focus for improvement. Discussion of the report helps school leaders understand what they can do to improve their school—insights that mere test scores don't provide.

Sadly, this very promising piloting of the School Quality Review concept was curtailed in New York state when the new State Education Commissioner, Richard Mills, replaced Thomas Sobel in 1997. Commissioner Mills has also announced that he does not support the idea of schools being able to establish their own graduation performance standards—insisting, instead, that all students must pass new state regents standardized tests in order to receive a New York high school diploma. New York, like many other states, has moved to a very limited, standardized—and test-driven—definition of school accountability.

While not officially sanctioned by the state, a committed group of educators in New York has continued to develop and refine the concepts of performance-based assessment of student work and professional development. The New York Performance Standards Consortium, which has thirty-nine high schools serving sixteen thousand students in its membership, has identified six tasks that all their students have to complete in order to graduate: a research paper, a literary essay, a scientific experiment, a real-life application of high-level mathematics, a creative work of art, and a written self-evaluation. They are also developing an external peer review process aimed at helping teachers to more accurately assess and improve student work and school leaders to reflect on the needed school improvements.

Two states, Rhode Island and Illinois, use what they call School Visits as an integral part of their accountability plan. Rhode Island State Education Commissioner Peter McWalters recently related a story in conversation that demonstrates the value of school reviews for even so-called good schools. After spending several days in one of the state's most prestigious high schools, the School Visiting Team reported that while this school had some of the highest test scores in the state—due in large part to the fact that its students, from predominantly privileged backgrounds, came into the ninth grade with high scores—they did not see significant evidence that the high school had "added value" for these students between ninth and twelfth grade. The school was riding on its reputation for high test scores, but according to the School Visiting Team, they were doing little to really challenge students.

ELEMENTS OF A MORE EFFECTIVE ACCOUNTABILITY SYSTEM

We are now at a point where we can begin to describe some of the qualities and characteristics of a more effective system of student and school accountability. The first issue we will consider is a theme to which we continue to return in this book: student and teacher motivation.

Formative versus Punitive Assessment

An effective accountability system in education cannot be just a game of "gotcha." A good system of accountability—whether for students or for schools—must not only accurately assess important strengths and weakness, but must also help provide the motivation and insight needed to improve. Our current testing systems fall short on both counts.

First, the tests do not often assess the competencies that are most important for work and citizenship. Second, the tests do not motivate learning. The requirement to teach to the test has a profoundly demoralizing influence on students and teachers alike. Worst of all, test results often are not available for at least six months or more after the tests have been taken. By the time a teacher gets his class's test scores, the students have moved on. And so the results cannot be used to modify teaching methods or curriculum in a timely fashion. And the tests themselves rarely give the kind of information about students' strengths and weaknesses that can help a teacher to know what to do differently. Students almost never find out what, specifically, they did right and wrong on these tests, either. In the final analysis, most of the standardized tests now in use do not inform the teaching and learning process. They merely punish poor-performing students and humiliate teachers.

What, then, might be the critical elements of a new kind of assessment and accountability system that motivates the desire to improve, while providing parents and community members with essential information about schools? What would a better system look like? Let me suggest five interdependent elements of an accountability system that meet these criteria more effectively than our current models.

1. "Authentic" Student Work Assessed through "Performances"

In the stories of Central Park East and the Chugach School District, we learned how a very different system of assessing student work could reshape the curriculum in ways that positively impact students' desire to learn as well as their levels of achievement. The work that students do in these places has intrinsic meaning. They know they are mastering competencies needed to be successful in the adult world. And their level of mastery is being constantly assessed through projects and exhibitions of their work, where they learn from their mistakes and apply what they learn to future work.

Consider, again, the comparison to scouting. What if you had to take multiple-choice tests on the parts of a tent and campfire to earn your camp skills merit badge? Imagine, too, that the test had a number of tricky questions—ones where there might be more than one right answer or that asked for obscure information. How motivated would you be in such an assessment system? And even if you passed the test, what would you really know? How competent would you be?

This is the essence of the standardized testing dilemma: it is an assessment system that neither motivates nor teaches. This is why the Boy Scouts don't use such tests. If you want to earn your camp skills badge, you have to demonstrate real knowledge and skills: Light the fire, pitch the tent!

As I have already mentioned, since the time of Socrates, the elites in many societies have been educated and assessed by these means: Make the speech, defend the thesis! At a time when we need all students to learn to use their minds well for both work and citizenship, why should we continue to rely on an obsolete and ineffectual system of assessment? When it comes to creating more sophisticated assessments of student work, we can do better, much better. And if we do, then students will too.

2. Multiple Measures of School "Success"

We have seen how standardized tests are problematic as a means of evaluating schools for both minority students and students from privileged backgrounds. Minority students from Central Park East, who perform poorly on certain standardized tests, nevertheless are graduating from high school with real competence, are going to college, and are doing well. On the other hand, the Rhode Island School Visiting Team discovered that students from an upper-middle-class community were being poorly served by their high school, despite its high test scores.

Insisting on more sophisticated ways of assessing student work will take us a long way toward establishing a basis for evaluating the quality of a school. As educators and parents learn what good student work looks like, they will bring fresh eyes and new skills to teams that review a school's portfolio. Just as student portfolios and performances of real tasks provide multiple measures of student mastery, so too can School Quality Reviews tell us far more about schools than just test scores alone. Through both qualitative and quantitative measures, they tell us about the quality of the work being done by both students and adults. They provide insight into the level of engagement. More importantly, such "peer review" provides real opportunities to generate new knowledge about what must be done to improve a school.

3. "Licensing" Public School Operators

But even with more sophisticated ways of determining school quality, we still must deal with the issue of accountability. Who should be the sponsoring agency for School Quality Reviews, and what should be done if the process determines that a school is not effective? Let me conclude this chapter with an outline of some of the key components for what could be a new comprehensive system of school accountability.

The issue of sanctions and safeguards for school quality is increasingly urgent as it becomes more clear that American public school districts are unable to improve the schools for which they are responsible. A growing number of individuals and organizations are beginning to question whether school districts, as we know them, are even capable of reforming themselves, and we will look at some of the reasons why this may be true in chapter 5.

Whatever groups may think about districts, nearly everyone agrees that urban high schools are the most resistant to change—even when they are given substantial additional resources by outside agencies. Meanwhile, individuals and groups are starting highly successful new public high schools in a number of cities—including New York, Philadelphia, and Chicago. The story of these efforts has been recently chronicled in the book *Creating New Schools: How Small Schools Are Changing American Education*, edited by Evans Clinchy.

In New York City alone, nearly sixty thousand children attend new small schools—schools similar in many respects to Central Park East, but sponsored by a wide range of education reform networks, community agencies, youth groups, and so on. Despite constant battles with district and state bureaucracies, these new schools have survived and do a dramatically better job of graduating students and getting them into college. So a growing number of people are beginning to ask: What kind of system could be put into place that would facilitate the creation of many more schools like Central Park East?

Paul T. Hill, director of the Center for Reinventing Education at the University of Washington, has laid the groundwork for the creation of a new system of public education accountability in his landmark book, *Reinventing Public Education*, which he coauthored with Lawrence C. Pierce and James W. Guthrie. His idea is elegantly simple: school districts should get out of the business of trying to manage vast systems of public schools and, instead, should become licensing agencies for individuals or groups who want to run public schools.

Under such a system, individuals or groups would apply for a license to run a public school. If successful, they would be granted a contract, which would spell out the kind of program to be provided, budgets, evaluation criteria, and so on. The contract would be for a limited term—say five years—and could only be renewed if the school "operator" was shown to be providing an effective program *and* was able to attract a clientele. Parents and students would be given complete choice of schools, as they are now in a number of urban school systems. But unlike the current system, where schools never "go out of business," if a school suffered a decline in population because it was not a popular provider in the marketplace, it would lose its license to operate.

A far-fetched idea? Elements of this education system have been used by the American system of private schools for most of this century. Operators of private schools do not have to apply for a license to run their school, but they do have to attract enough customers to remain in business and be accredited. As we saw earlier in this chapter, regional school accreditation associations set standards and enforce them through periodic school visits. This "chartering" or licensing mechanism is also how Massachusetts and a number of other states are legislating the existence of public charter schools. Finally, the nonpartisan Education Commission of the States recently published a report that spells out in some detail how such a new governance system might work and what kinds of enabling legislation would be needed.[7]

4. "Licensing" Standards

Just as the role of districts and school boards would have to change fundamentally in order for such a system to work, so too would the role of the states. States have to get out of the business of creating one single set of academic standards and accompanying tests—a job most informed observers agree is being done very poorly. Instead, states must be in the new business of being a *Consumer Reports* for education.

Through the creation of mandatory academic standards, states are increasingly regulating their public schools' curriculum. The impact on schools is to create more and more uniformity. In Massachusetts, for example, charter schools were given total discretion with respect to curriculum under the 1993 Education Reform Act, in return for the greater accountability of having to apply for license (or charter) renewal every five years. But the same law took away much of that freedom by legislating the creation of new state education standards and tests. Now that these new standards are in place, charter and other public school educators are told by the state both *what* must be taught in different subjects and *when*.

Let me cite an example from experience. Many humanities teachers believe students gain a much deeper understanding of American culture by studying American history and literature at the same time—and even more so when teachers in each course attempt to interrelate the content of history and literature. American studies courses are often offered in high schools honors tracks and in elite colleges as well. The teachers of City On A Hill Charter School, where I was a founding trustee, set out to create such a demanding curriculum for its urban minority students.

But now in Massachusetts, that approach to curriculum is no longer possible. The state has determined that American literature is to be studied in ninth and tenth grade, along with world history, while American history (and world literature) is studied in eleventh grade. Any school that ignores this state requirement is putting its school's tenth grade standardized test scores at risk, as they test the specified curriculum content. And so City On A Hill Charter School had to revamp its curriculum to be in alignment with state standards, even though teachers there do not think the new state approach is as effective as the one they had developed.

In fact, we have no evidence whatsoever that one particular set of academic standards—or indeed even the existence of state-mandated academic standards—significantly improves student achievement. Why, then, should we allow politicians and a handful of academic content "experts" and test-makers to determine the curriculum for every public school student in a state?

Rather than being in the business of creating and administering academic standards and accompanying tests, I propose that states license multiple academic standards providers in the same way that Paul Hill proposes having districts license school operators.

In fact, we already have a number of organizations that have developed excellent—but different—academic content standards and accompanying curricula and assessments. In the for-profit sector, there is the Edison Project and the Sylvan Learning Systems. In the nonprofit world, many of the original New American Schools partners have created outstanding curricula, as have other national school reform organizations. We have also seen earlier in this chapter that networks of schools and individual districts like Chugach can and do create outstanding sets of standards and accompanying curricula.

Different parents want different things for their children. Some want a very traditional curriculum, where memorization is emphasized. Others want a much more project-based "thinking" curriculum. We all agree we need more rigor in schools—but in fact many of us have different definitions of what is considered academically rigorous. Why should citizens in a state be given only one way to learn, only one curriculum? Why not give public school parents the same variety of choices of approaches to learning that parents who send their children to private schools have in many communities?

If states got completely out of the business of creating academic standards and developing and administering more and more tests, they would have significant additional resources to research and "certify" various packages of academic standards for use in their public schools. There would also be new money for state-sponsored School Quality Review Teams, which would provide essential information to education consumers and to the new district public school licensing agencies. The result of these two state efforts would be to create more real choices of high-quality approaches to teaching and learning and much more in-depth information about the characteristics of individual schools and their track records.

5. A National Literacy and Numeracy Test

While I have argued against various forms of standardized testing throughout this book, I am not opposed to all standardized tests. My view is that a student and school accountability system, which is based entirely on cheap, multiple-choice standardized tests, undermines real learning, as well as the motivation of both students and teachers to improve. Most of the state tests now used do not measure the thinking, information synthesis, and problem-solving skills that are essential for work and citizenship, and their excessive use profoundly demoralizes students and teachers alike.

High-quality standardized tests do have a role as a part of a more sophisticated accountability system, however. We do need some data about student learning that we can use to look at schools in different districts or even in different states comparatively. We also need tests that give us good diagnostic information about students' learning. Let me briefly outline what I think the parameters of such a system should be.

First, such tests cannot be developed by individual states—not only because of the politicization of local decision making, but also for a very practical reason. With each state developing its own tests, there is no simple way to compare student achievement data across states. So you have a situation where a state like Louisiana, for example, proclaimed very high literacy rates for years, according to its own state-administered test, at a time when most employers would not move operations there because the state's workforce was substantially illiterate.

In response to growing criticism, states have recently moved to administering two different sets of tests. Most have their own "home-grown" tests, which are supposed to be aligned to their state's academic standards. Then they also administer a nationally recognized "norm-referenced" test, such as the Stanford 9 or the Iowa Test of Basic Skills, which claims to give national comparative data. Thus, more and more school days are taken up with testing, instead of learning, and there is no end in sight.

I think the solution is simple: there should be one national test, instead of forty-nine (Iowa has none) state tests and dozens of national tests that must also be administered to validate the results of the state tests. In fact, we already have such tests, the NAEP. And while there is some controversy about the scale the National Governing Board uses to score the tests, as we have seen, the actual tests are generally well regarded.

However, the NAEP tests need to be improved in several essential respects. First and most important, teachers and schools must get test scores in a timely fashion so that they can use the results to diagnose student learning deficiencies. Tom Vander Ark, executive director of the Bill & Melinda Gates Foundation Education Initiative, has proposed the creation of a system of online literacy and numeracy testing at every grade level so that teachers and students alike can get instant results and track progress easily. There are several national reading curriculums that have this feature, and teachers report that it is invaluable.

Second, I think the content of NAEP numeracy or math tests needs to be reexamined in light of the math skills most needed today. Very few of us will ever need to use advanced algebra in our adult lives, but we all need to understand probability, statistics, and methods of measurement—as well as practical skills such as how to fill a tax form and create a budget. NAEP tests can also include more performance-based assessments. While not every student could be required as a part of NAEP testing to give an oral presentation in every school every year because of cost factors, as an example, NAEP could move in the direction of periodically sampling and scoring student performances of this kind. The message to teachers would be that what students can do with knowledge matters more than their performance on fill-in-the-bubble questions.

The argument often made against a national test is that it will lead to the creation of a national curriculum. However, that is only a problem if the test is constructed around a specific body of academic material. The best NAEP test is probably the one that measures skills in reading and writing at different grade levels. It is an assessment of intellectual proficiencies, not mastery of a specific body of material. It does not tell students what they are supposed to read. The solution to the fear of a "national curriculum," then, is to test only literacy and numeracy competencies. Decisions about the content of the science or social studies standards—which are always the most controversial—would be up to individual schools, whose standards would be certified by the state and assessed through a School Quality Review process.

Another safeguard against a national curriculum is to create more performance-based components of NAEP. The best tests are inherently "curriculum proof" in that they do not have questions about things that can be memorized the night before. They test competencies developed over time, using a variety of approaches.

Testing CQ: A Common Civics Curriculum

We may want to consider specifying the parameters of the secondary national literacy test, however, so that questions draw from and assume some knowledge of civics and develop what I call citizenship intelligence, or CQ. Instead of asking students to write about a quote from a work of literature or a "topical" issue, why not create different essay questions each year that ask students to interpret a passage from the Declaration of Independence or one of the constitutional amendments? Additional essay questions might ask students to write about a time in their lives when they were involved in community service or stood up for an idea or issue that was important to them. In this way, we could create some basic expectations about a common citizenship curriculum for all Americans.

There is nothing wrong with teaching to a test—as long as it is a good one that assesses carefully things we consider most important.

CREATING A "PRIVATE" PUBLIC EDUCATION SYSTEM

These days there is a great deal of controversy over the idea of giving families "vouchers"—a fixed sum of money—which they could spend on the private or parochial school of their choice. Essentially, the proposal is an attempt to fix our system of public education by creating more of a free enterprise marketplace. If the new Republican administration has its way, voucher systems will become a core element of public education. However, proponents of the plan do not talk very much about how the private and parochial schools would be held accountable. Private school students generally are not required to take state education tests, and the National Association of Independent Schools vehemently opposes vouchers because they fear the increased government regulation of private schools that vouchers will likely mean.

A voucher system, then, would either be completely unregulated or it would eventually be regulated by the same system now in place for existing public schools—state-mandated curricula and high-stakes standardized tests for all. My hunch is that even the most ardent proponents of vouchers would be unhappy with this state monopoly of academic standards, and most private school clientele would not stand for it.

The solution, I believe, is not a voucher plan, but rather making our public education accountability systems more like those that exist in the elite private schools. To assess what students know, the best private schools and colleges don't used standardized tests very much, if at all. And few of their teachers rely solely on multiple-choice exams. Projects, essays, and oral exams are the most common forms of testing—because they are the best measure of what students really can do with knowledge. Why shouldn't we have this same system in our public schools?

In many parts of this country, private schools differ greatly from one another in curriculum and educational philosophy. Parents choose the program that they believe best matches the needs and interests of their children. Here in the Boston area where I live, assuming I had the money for tuition, I could have sent my children to a parochial or private school where kids sit in rows and wear uniforms, or one that emphasizes sports or the arts, or a school where kids call their teachers by their first names and spend much of their day on project-based work. All of these schools are fully accredited and would have provided a decent education. All of them get students into college, where they perform well. Why shouldn't we have these same choices in public schools?

Independent schools long ago discovered the power of peer review, as well as the discipline of the marketplace. Through these two mechanisms, they are largely self-regulating—and are a successful system for the most part. Why can't we reduce the bureaucratization of public education accountability systems—which have not worked—in favor of a new, more flexible accountability system?

Why can't all students have some of the benefits of an education system that only the elites now enjoy? If the system is good enough for the wealthy, then why won't it work for the rest of us? Why do we need to give vouchers to families to leave public education in favor of private schools? Why not make our public schools more like the private schools instead?

There are, of course, obvious differences between public and private schools. Private schools don't have to take all students, and we know that in many public schools today, low-income and minority students are receiving little or no real education. And so the kind of accountability system I am proposing has some new features and safeguards—like school licensing, state-sponsored School Quality Review Teams and certification of standards, and a national test.

But in many respects the essence of what I am proposing is similar to the accountability system we've used in both private and public New Village

Schools for many hundreds of years. It works on a small scale—far better than the government-regulated bureaucratic solutions we now use. It's time to see if we can make face-to-face, New Village School accountability work for all students.

For such a system to work well, however, we need a better understanding of what makes a good school—besides test scores. What do good schools where all students and their teachers are challenged and motivated to do their best look like—and how are these schools different from most of the "assembly-line" factory schools we have today?

These are some of the questions we consider in the next chapter.

4

WHAT DO "GOOD SCHOOLS" LOOK LIKE?

Throughout this book, winning the hearts and minds of students and teachers—motivating excellence—has been a recurring theme. In the Introduction, I described how labeling the educational problem today as simply an issue of "failing" schools is a fundamental distortion of the facts, which has a profoundly demoralizing effect on teachers. In chapter 1, I described how today's students are no longer as motivated by the incentives for learning that influenced many previous generations: fear and respect for authority and the belief in "success" as the reward for years of hard work and delayed gratification. In this chapter, I also discussed how young people's increasing isolation from the adult world makes it far harder for them to understand what "membership" in that world requires.

In chapters 2 and 3, we learned that an emphasis on mastery and assessment of real competencies helps teachers to focus on what is most important and enables students to better understand the value of what they are learning. In the last chapter, we also learned how Deborah Meier's school, Central Park East Secondary School, pioneered a system of assessment that motivated students to take on more challenging work and, ultimately, to achieve greater levels of academic competence. We looked at its requirements of exhibitions of mastery through oral and written work in fourteen different areas for graduation. We learned how successful the school has been, with almost every student graduating and more than 90 percent going on to college—in a city school system that graduates only about 50 percent of its high school students and where few go on for further learning.

THE NEW VILLAGE SCHOOL

The fact that students have to master real competencies in order to graduate—rather than merely serve "seat time"—is an important factor in motivating students, I believe. But it is far from the only factor. Central Park East created a new model for a grade 7–12 school—one that "breaks the mold" of American public middle and high schools in many respects. It has become a model for a generation of educational entrepreneurs who are creating their own new small middle and high schools. For all of these reasons, it is important, then, to take a closer look at the Central Park East model and to understand the elements that contribute to fundamental differences in both student and teacher motivation, in comparison to more traditional junior and senior high schools.

But first, a disclaimer. I am not holding up Central Park East as *the* model school. Nor do I think the school is perfect, and it is probably not now the same as it was when Deborah Meier was principal. Rather, my intention is to explore some of the features of the school that have made a significant difference in the lives of both students and teachers. In the final analysis, Central Park East is an example of what can happen when educators engage in research and development to invent better schools. Deborah Meier would be one of the first to agree that successive generations who build on this pioneering work will, no doubt, improve on the prototype.

SEVEN FACTORS INFLUENCING STUDENT MOTIVATION

Meier believes that the goal of high school reform should be to make all high schools more like our best elementary schools. In a very conscious way, many of the "design" elements of Central Park East Secondary School are influenced by what Meier learned through years of teaching and, later, leading outstanding elementary schools. In the following analysis, I have identified seven characteristics of CPESS (and many other successful secondary schools) that I believe are central to motivating all students to want to achieve at high academic levels.[1]

1. Teachers Know Their Students Well

Meier's thinking about high schools was influenced by the work of Ted Sizer and his colleagues at the Coalition of Essential Schools, where Central Park East was a charter member. One of the most important principles of the school is, in fact, best summarized in one of Sizer's succinct aphorisms and lies at the very heart of the motivation issue for students today: "You can't motivate a student you don't know."

While on paper the typical high school or junior high school has an 18:1 student-to-teacher ratio, in fact most teacher see an average of a 150 students a day—for a semester or perhaps a year. The next year, teachers start over, trying to get to know the names of another 150 or so students. And in between classes, five or six times a day, students and teachers alike become anonymous and lost in the vast ocean of bodies that flows down the hallways of our typical high schools that enroll anywhere from fifteen hundred to four thousand students. In many of these schools, teachers don't even know the names of all their colleagues—let alone their students.

Remember our discussion of the growing isolation of young people from adults in chapter 1? When high school students are asked to name the single most important change that might be made which would improve their learning, the overwhelming majority say, "having teachers who know me and who care about me."[2] Meeting this demand is simply not possible in our large junior and senior high schools, as they're presently organized.

The trick is to think out of the box—and to make student-teacher relationships the top priority. Central Park East consciously set out to create a much smaller school. To do so, they developed a unique class schedule and used their instructional budget very differently than most schools—as we'll see.

Central Park East enrolls about 450 students in grades 7–12—a size that Meier considers too large, although it is less than half the size of an average grade 9–12 high school. It shares an old public school building in Harlem with two other schools. The school is divided into "houses" of seventy-five to eighty students and four teachers. Teachers typically teach more than one subject—such as English and history, and they teach the subjects together as an interdisciplinary course over a much longer period of time in the day. The structure is more like that of an elementary school, with teachers spending much longer blocks of time with a group of students. Teams of teachers also work with the same group of students for two years.

The class sizes and student load of teachers is further reduced by the fact that almost everyone teaches at Central Park East—even the principal. There are no nonteaching administrators or "specialists" who, in a typical school district, can consume as much as half of the total personnel budget. The final result: teachers see an average of only about forty students per day—much closer to a typical elementary school than a high school. And this is accomplished at virtually the same per student cost as large comprehensive schools.[3]

What difference does this make for teachers and students? In a word, everything. For teachers, the benefits are obvious. They come to understand each student's academic strengths and weakness deeply. Teachers can get to know each student's individual interests as well. The curriculum, then, is a mixture of students' academic needs and personal interests, and it is often highly individualized. Teachers can tailor assignments to individual student learning levels to a great extent—without having to create separate academic tracks for students.

There is a further advantage to knowing students well in the team structure of the school. Because four teachers share the same group of seventy-five or so students, they can and do get together regularly to talk about how individual students are doing in different classes, and what more might be done. There are no cracks for students to fall through in this school. When asked how CPESS is different from other schools they've attended, students answer the question in very similar ways, "People care about me here." One young woman explained further, "If I've had a bad fight with my mom the night before, and I come to school bummed, someone notices right away. They say, 'Hey, Sonia, you don't look good. What's the matter?' I'm a real person at this school, instead of a number."

2. The Curriculum Is Intellectually Challenging and Engaging

Many schools pride themselves on creating a "caring" environment, like the one I've just described. I've worked with many teachers in inner-city and rural schools and in programs for emotionally handicapped children who say their most important job is to bolster kids' "self-esteem." But while these well-meaning teachers may tell students how special they are, if they have not given students real intellectual competencies, what self-esteem students may have acquired will quickly evaporate when they find themselves without skills and marginally employed in the adult world.

Caring and competence, respect and rigor. They are inseparable. Caring is not enough by itself, but you cannot motivate students to achieve competence if you do not care. You won't get rigor without real respect.

The other side of the equation is often equally problematic: many teachers' definitions of "intellectual rigor" are as out of touch as the definitions of self-esteem I just described. Most students complain that so-called academically rigorous college prep high school courses are incredibly boring and irrelevant to their present and future lives. Even many of the kids who do well in these courses—in hopes of getting into a "good" college—complain about the lack of challenge and the incredible amount of trivia they are asked to memorize—most of which they forget as soon as the test is over.

Many of the same people who decide what gets tested—college-level academic content specialists—also write the textbooks that shape the content of most high school academic courses. Their definition of what is "academically rigorous" is highly colored by their own school and college experiences and subject content expertise. "Guild" membership—credentialing of the few folks who get to write the textbooks—is tightly controlled by Ph.D. programs, which inculcate students into studying highly abstruse and often irrelevant subjects.

I will never forget a meeting with the professor in charge of my program area during my first year of doctoral work at Harvard. I expressed a desire to write a dissertation that would be truly useful to practitioners. "But that wouldn't be a worthwhile study," she said. "Your dissertation should be a conversation with just a few people in the world around an area of very specific expertise." Through conversations with doctoral students in many academic disciplines, I have found that my experience was typical. Fortunately, I eventually found a few professors who valued research on topics of more general interest to educators, and I wrote a dissertation about how schools change, which was the basis for my first book.

Sadly, the "halls of academia" have become very far removed, if not entirely separated, from the interests and needs of many thoughtful and curious people. The very term "academic" has become synonymous with "*irrelevant in practice:* theoretical and not of any practical relevance," a definition given for the word in a widely used dictionary.[4]

The content of "academic" subjects is only half the problem, though. The other half is how it is usually delivered. Whether it is because many high school teachers would like to think of themselves as college professors or because they simply don't know any other teaching methods, the overwhelming majority lectures endlessly. And they rarely engage their students in real discussions. In his famous study of high schools, John Goodlad found that the one constant in high school classrooms around the country is how much teachers talked—more than 70 percent of the class time on average.[5]

The result of both the content and the delivery of academic subjects is that many students "turn off" to all learning at a very young age. Knowing this all too well, Meier and her teachers set out to create an intellectually challenging curriculum—one that would prepare students for college but would be far more essential and engaging that the traditional "college-prep" courses.

As we saw in the discussion of the merit badge approach to learning, the teachers at CPESS focus on teaching and assessing habits of mind. The Central Park East five habits of mind, which were developed by Meier and her teachers over time, are:

- *Weighing evidence:* How do we know what we know? What is the evidence and is it credible?

- *Awareness of varying viewpoints:* What viewpoint are we hearing, seeing, reading? Who is the author and what are his/her intentions?

- *Seeing connections and relationships:* How are things connected to each other? Where have we heard or seen this before?

- *Speculating on possibilities:* What if . . . ? Can we imagine alternatives?

- *Assessing value both socially and personally:* What difference does it make? Who cares?

Every student takes the same core subjects at CPESS, and they are often taught as interdisciplinary classes that meet in two-hour blocks. Teachers rarely lecture. Socratic dialogue is the most common form of instruction. The courses have a great deal of academic content, but the content is organized around exploration of "essential questions," rather than a textbook's division of knowledge, and the goal of the course is furthering the habits of mind outlined above.

A seventh-grader's humanities/social studies class, for example, is organized around the theme of the emergence of contemporary political issues. The essential questions that drive the yearlong curriculum, which includes reading novels as well as primary and secondary historical documents, include:

- How do people achieve power?
- How do people respond to being deprived of power?
- How does power change hands?
- What gives laws their power?

The seventh- and eighth-grade science curriculum is similarly organized around a list of essential questions, such as who and what we are, how we work, and how we fit into the environment. This class is taught back-to-back with a math class for the same students—a schedule that allows for greater flexibility, as well as some integration of subject content.

Although there are no electives at CPESS, students have a great deal of choice when it comes to preparing papers and projects that demonstrate mastery in individual courses and their graduation portfolio. These research papers and projects are the primary means by which students are evaluated and are integral to what motivates students to take on challenging academic work. Students who have done independent research or projects in traditional schools will tell you they both learn more from these efforts and find them much more engaging than anything in their regular classes.

3. A Student's "Voice" Is Encouraged

It isn't just the challenging questions and choice of projects and topics for papers that motivates students at CPESS, I think. It is also the fact that students are strongly encouraged to develop their own "voice" in their work.

Evidence of student "voice" is everywhere. In discussions, students are expected to develop their opinions and interpretations, based on reason or evidence. Students' writing is characterized by the development of firm opinions and by the ways in which they relate "academic" topics to personal experiences and interests. The walls of the classrooms and hallways are covered with examples of good student writing and research papers, math projects with graphing and charts, artwork of every kind. The classrooms look much more like elementary school classrooms than conventional high school rooms.

When Meier refers to "the power of their ideas"—the title of her book about the school—she is expressing her conviction and her experience that all students can have powerful ideas and are worth hearing. There are regular class and whole school meetings where students discuss current issues, voice concerns, and argue for changes in the school. Adults listen and respond without being condescending. Students' opinions and ideas are taken seriously at every level. Indeed, the development of "student voice"—students' individual and unique construction of knowledge—may be the only way real learning occurs. The famous Swiss developmental psychologist Jean Piaget said it another way: "To understand is to invent." Student voice is student invention—thoughtfully critiqued by caring and informed adults.

4. Students Have Opportunities for "Real-World" Learning

Students have many opportunities to learn out of the classroom at CPESS. The small size and structure of the school enable teachers to more easily take field trips than in conventional schools, and the curriculum emphasizes "real-world" applications.

But more than just having frequent field trip opportunities, "real-world" learning is a requirement at Central Park East Secondary School. First of all, every student is released from classes to do a half-day of community service each week. Meier confessed to me in a recent conversation that she originally created the community service program primarily to give teacher teams additional planning time, but she quickly came to discover powerful benefits for students as well.

For many students, performing community service in various agencies is an opportunity to learn what kinds of skills are needed in the adult world. It is also a chance to make connections with adults who can serve as big brothers or sisters and mentors. A national organization called City Year has also found that giving adolescents and young adults a chance to "make a difference" through a year of community service develops leadership and both CQ and EQ skills, while teaching tolerance and respect for differences. Evaluation studies show that the program has a profound effect on participants' rates of involvement in civic affairs years after they've graduated from the program.[6]

Work internships are another way students at CPESS learn in the real world. Most students also take one or more classes at a local college in the final years at the school, which is an opportunity for a student to pursue a particular intellectual interest, while getting an introduction to demands of college life. As we learned in the last chapter, all students must complete a postgraduate plan and a project based on one or more work or service experiences in order to graduate.

5. Students Have an Emotional "Support System"

We've observed that Central Park East promotes closer adult-student relationships in a number of ways. Small classes and two years spent with the same teacher enable all teachers to know every student well. Students also have opportunities to forge meaningful relationships with adults outside of school through their community service projects and work internships. But Meier and her colleagues did not stop there. They created an "advisory program" for all students, adapted from an idea developed by Dennis Littky at the Thayer High School.

Students spend an average of an hour a day with their advisory group. In Meier's words, the advisory time is "a combination tutorial, seminar, and study hall." Of course, it is a time for students to get extra help or to complete work, but it is also much more. Advisory meetings are a time to talk about current events, health education, and school issues. They are also the way in which the school handles college advising. In fact, advisory groups often take trips to visit colleges together. Since every professional adult in the building has an advisory group, there are no more than fifteen students in a group.

My observation is that advisory groups become a kind of extended family. They provide an opportunity for students to forge close relationships with a caring adult as well as with peers—an opportunity that is all too often missing for an increasing number of adolescents who spend the majority of their waking hours alone. If a student misses a class or is struggling with a personal issue—either in or out of school—an adult who knows that student well hears about the problem and can offer help immediately.

6. The School Forges Close Ties to Parents

Many secondary educators complain about the lack of parental involvement in their schools, but few have taken the time to really look at obstacles to parental involvement created by the very structure of most schools. Parents in minority and/or economically disadvantaged communities often start with a skepticism, at best, or even a fear of people—usually white—who hold institutional power. For many of them, school was not a particularly happy experience or a place where they felt successful. So just to step through the doorway of a school building requires an act of faith or even courage for some families.

The circumstances in which parents and educators are thrown together often make the problem worse. Teachers in conventional schools, as we have seen, have little time to get to know students well. They have too many and they see them for only a small snippet of time in the day. When parents show up for the once-a-year perfunctory "back-to-school" night, teachers have little to share about individual students—and no time in which to do it. The typical back-to-school night schedule in junior and senior high schools asks parents to shuffle from class to class every ten minutes or so, in a desperate attempt to give them glimpses of all of their children's teachers.

The so-called guidance system offers little help to parents in middle and high schools. Guidance counselors typically have a student load of four hundred to nine hundred students. They are often simply glorified schedulers who do not have time to get to know students—despite the good intentions of many. Often, only when a child gets into trouble are families called in for a one-on-one conference.

With these few "opportunities" for parental involvement—other than serving on a PTA committee, for which few people have time—is it really surprising that many parents don't want any part of their children's school? The experience for parents is often as dehumanizing as it is for their children.

Being a former elementary teacher, Meier understands the importance of parental involvement—especially family support for academic achievement. Far from being a replacement for family, the existence of a faculty advisor is at the heart of the school's strategy to strengthen ties between families and the school. The advisor—someone who knows the student well—is the primary point of contact between a student's parents or guardian and the school. Three times a year the school holds parent-advisor-student conferences lasting at least a half hour. The advisor and the student together talk about the student's work—what's going well, what's most interesting, what needs improvement, and how the parent or guardian can help. Once again, the model for CPESS is much closer to what elementary schools do.

The result: virtually 100 percent attendance. Students and their families both look forward to the conferences.

7. The School Provides a Safe and Respectful Environment

Adolescents at CPESS and other similar schools sometimes complain about the extent to which adults "know their business" or are "in their face." But what they give up in anonymity, students more than gain back in a sense of safety and belonging.

Advisory groups help to establish strong norms of behavior—less through formal rules than through loyalties to relationships that matter a great deal to students. Students come to respect and care for one another in ways that are very different from conventional schools. One result is that life-threatening violence is almost unheard of at CPESS, and discipline is a comparatively minor problem—in contrast to traditional high schools where enforcing rules is the full-time occupation of at least several adults.

Relationships with teachers, as we have seen, are also profoundly different. Students feel "heard" and deeply respected by all adults. Parents feel respected as well. Respect and trust are explicit core values of the school and are a direct result of its structure. The school is a community created at a scale that allows people to know each other well. Meier quotes noted African-American author Henry Louis Gates: "There is no tolerance without respect—and no respect without knowledge."

WHAT MOTIVATES TEACHERS, AND WHAT INVESTMENTS IN TEACHING MIGHT IMPROVE STUDENT LEARNING?

Before we talk about the factors in the Central Park East design that positively influence teacher motivation, we first need to dispel two myths about what motivates teachers and what kinds of investments in teacher training are most likely to improve student learning.

Many in our society believe that teachers are underpaid, and so they are when their jobs are compared to others requiring a comparable education. But then leading "experts," union leaders, and policy makers alike go on to assume that teachers' desire for better salaries can be a motivator for improving student achievement. The idea seems simple and noncontroversial: link increases in teachers' salaries to improvements in students' test scores.

The second common belief is that student achievement is low because teachers are poorly prepared. If teachers were required to earn a master's degree and had more professional development, the reasoning goes, then student achievement would go up.

These beliefs are widespread. Instituting "merit pay," recruiting more highly trained teachers, and giving them more on-the-job training are, in fact, leading strategies that many schools and districts currently use to improve student test scores and achievement. But two important studies suggest that any effort to improve student learning using these strategies alone is likely to fail.

The "Higher Salary" Myth

In her book *Teachers at Work*, Susan Moore Johnson documented important differences in the rates of job satisfaction between private versus public school teachers. She found that private school teachers were much more satisfied with their jobs than their colleagues in public school, *despite the fact that they earned significantly less.* Johnson went on to describe some of the fundamental differences in the working conditions in the two kinds of schools and how these affected teacher morale.

This study was completed before the onslaught of high-stakes testing. In the last ten years, public school teacher morale has declined dramatically, as we discussed earlier in this book. A recently released Public Agenda Foundation study, *A Sense of Calling,* supplements Johnson's study with a wealth of new data. The following table summarizes several stark differences in the morale of private versus public school teachers:[7]

	PRIVATE SCHOOL TEACHERS	PUBLIC SCHOOL TEACHERS
Their job gives them a sense that they are respected and appreciated	86%	66%
They can count on parental support	54%	20%
Teachers' morale is high at their school	49%	28%

The morale of both private and public school teachers is not high, but it is significantly less in public schools. The Public Agenda Foundation study explored whether low wages were a factor and to what extent salary increases would improve morale when compared with other changes that might be made in teachers' working conditions. The results startled many policy pundits and business leaders, who assume that everyone is motivated by the desire for more money.

The question Public Agenda asked was: "Given a choice between two schools in otherwise identical districts, which would you prefer to work in?" The results are summarized in the following table:

	PUBLIC SCHOOL TEACHERS
The school with a significantly higher salary	12%
or	
The school where student behavior and parent support were significantly better	86%
The school with a significantly higher salary	17%
or	
The school where administrators gave strong backing and support to teachers	82%
The school with a significantly higher salary	23%
or	
The school with teachers who were highly motivated and effective	77%
The school with a significantly higher salary	25%
or	
The school whose academic mission and teaching philosophy you share	74%

Obviously, most teachers believe they deserve salaries comparable to other professionals, and, no doubt, morale would improve if both salaries and working conditions were better. However, what Public Agenda discovered is that teachers are far more motivated by "a sense of calling" than by any financial considerations. Most became teachers because they wanted to make a difference in students' lives, and what they most wanted were changes in their work environment that would enable them to be more effective.

The "Teacher Preparation" Myth

Given the assumption of many policy makers that improvements in teacher preparation are the cures for poor student achievement, another issue the Public Agenda report set out to explore in this study was the extent to which new teachers felt adequately trained. In fact, the vast majority of new teachers—71 percent—felt generally well-prepared for their new careers, but not for the working conditions they experienced.

Almost 60 percent of the teachers surveyed said that upon entering the profession, they did not know how to best help the lowest achieving students. However, the majority did not blame their training. Nearly three-quarters (73 percent) of the teachers surveyed agreed that "talented teachers are not enough on their own" to turn around the performance of low-achieving students, prompting the authors of the study to observe that, "The frustration of simply not being able to get though to some kids, to help them progress, takes a calculable—and debilitating—toll on teachers."

What changes do teachers think will help them be more effective? As we learned from the last table, many believe that parental support, effective leadership, and motivated colleagues are crucial attributes of an effective school—and are much more important than a higher salary. When asked to name a "very effective" way to improve teacher quality, "reducing class size" was at the top of the list—with 86 percent of the teachers surveyed agreeing. Only about half of the teachers surveyed thought that more professional development opportunities would improve teacher quality, a view that we will explore in the next section. The authors of the Public Agenda report warned that, "who becomes a teacher seems less of a problem than what happens to them once they enter a classroom. In the rush to improve education for the nation's youngsters, policymakers may do well to revisit their assumptions of what is wrong."

Support for this point of view comes from another new study as well. The Rand Corporation recently completed a state-by-state comparison of a decade of math test scores on the NAEP (among the forty-four states participating). The study reports significant differences among the levels of improvement between states when similar student populations are compared and then analyzes some of the investments that appear most and least effective in state efforts to improve student math achievement. The results surprised even the authors themselves.[8] *Education Week* reported some of the key findings of the study:

> The state-by-state analysis by the RAND Corp. also shows that some states and strategies are better than others in raising scores. Smaller class sizes, better resources for teachers, and preschool programs are linked to higher achievement, the report says, while the academic payoff from having higher-paid, more experienced, or more educated teachers appears less certain. . . .
>
> What didn't make an impact on a state's student performance, the researchers found, were teachers' salary levels, their years of experience, or the percentage of teachers with a master's degree.[9]

In the authors' own words, "efforts to increase the quality of teachers in the long run are important, but . . . significant productivity gains can be obtained with the current teaching force if their working conditions are improved."

There is one final aspect of the teacher preparation myth that must be addressed—the widely shared belief that teachers are less bright than other college graduates. You know the old—and hurtful—saying "those who can, do; those who can't, teach." While it is true that high school graduates who say they plan to go into education generally have lower SAT scores than those choosing other occupations, no studies have been done of those who actually finish college and become licensed to teach—until just recently. A new Educational Testing Service study concludes:

> Prospective teachers who earn licenses to practice have higher SAT scores than most college-bound high school seniors, according to a study released here at the recent annual meeting of the American Association of Colleges for Teacher Education.
>
> College-bound seniors who say they want to major in education have lower scores than their peers—an often-lamented fact. But the SAT scores of prospective teachers who actually seek licenses are nearly equal to those of all college-bound seniors, the study found, and scores for people who meet state licensing requirements exceed those of their peers.[10]

In summary, I do agree that teachers deserve a wage that is at least comparable to what other professionals receive, and I also know that teachers need ongoing opportunities for professional development—although not the kind they usually receive, as we'll soon see. But these are not the only critical factors that are most likely to improve teacher morale and student achievement. Unless we pay much more attention to the working conditions of teachers, they will not be motivated to want to learn new skills. We must pay as much attention to improving the *conditions* of both teaching and learning as we do to improving the *capacities* of educators.

What do teachers' working conditions and professional development look like, then, in a good school? Once more, we learn some important lessons from our New Village School—Central Park East.

FOUR FACTORS INFLUENCING TEACHER MOTIVATION

In the last section, teachers cited parental support, effective and supportive leadership, and motivated colleagues as essential "quality of work life" attributes. And we have already learned that one of the basic goals of Central Park East was to forge meaningful partnerships with parents. Strong leadership and colleagueship were also evident, but they were supported by four design elements of the school that I think are crucial in motivating teachers to continue to improve the quality of their work and effectiveness with students.

1. Time to Work Together

When teachers have a chance to reflect on the changes that have taken place in our world and are asked to think about how they might make their schools better, the first response you often hear is, "I agree we need to do that, but when are we going to do it? We have no time."

The typical school schedule is 8:30 A.M. to 3:30 P.M. Teachers spend about five of those hours teaching classes every day. They usually have some administrative tasks—like hall monitoring or lunch room duty—that take up another forty-five minutes on average, and then they have about the same amount of time for lesson planning, grading papers, and so on. That leaves half an hour in the regular day to eat lunch, have conferences with students, call parents, and take care of personal business. Many teachers come to school an hour or so early to do some of this work and also take home anywhere between an hour and three hours of work to do in the evening.

Perhaps once or twice a month at most, teachers are required to attend a faculty meeting lasting half an hour or so. Most of the time in these meetings is taken up with administrators talking at teachers about mundane organizational matters—scheduling, information about upcoming events, and so on—that could easily be communicated in writing. Then, perhaps two or three times a year, teachers have what districts call an "in-service" program—usually a district-mandated daylong session on a theme or topic of particular interest to the district at the moment. One day might be devoted to how to use the district's new report card, while the next is likely to be spent on a completely different topic, such as information about an anti-drug program.

These are the critical elements in the professional life of most public school teachers in this country. "Professional development" for most teachers has simply become a euphemism for another form of bureaucratic command and control, where administrators and outside "experts" tell teachers what education "leaders" think they need to know. This pattern of adult learning looks remarkably like the typical models of passive student learning—a problem that we will explore further in the last chapter.

What's missing from this picture? What is good "professional development"? Let me offer a concise answer: it is time for in-depth, ongoing adult dialogue and inquiry around issues of generally agreed-upon professional importance. Adults in schools need the same kinds of powerful "constructivist" learning opportunities that students need.

It is interesting to me that we tout Japan's high test scores, but we have made little effort to learn *how* they have achieved those scores or to adopt their most successful strategies. Several recent studies document that Japanese teachers typically spend only about half of their professional day teaching students. Instead, they spend several hours a day on intensive professional development that is largely peer driven and focused on improving teaching. An important new book by James Stigler and James Hiebert, *The Teaching Gap*, describes this "secret weapon" of Japanese school improvement. It is something they call the "lesson study" process. Small groups of teachers work together to identify particular learning problems in their classes and then collaboratively develop, test, and refine new lessons aimed at solving that learning problem. Successful results are then widely disseminated.

To my knowledge, Central Park East Secondary School did not have a system as formal as the lesson study process, but they did build much more time into the school day for teachers to talk together about their work. All faculty and staff meet together about four hours a week, on average, at CPESS. In addition, teaching teams met for at least another two hours or so every week—usually when students were off working on community service. Summarizing the importance of making this professional time an integral part of the school structure, Meier writes, "The kinds of changes required by today's (education reform) agenda can only be the work of thoughtful teachers. Either we acknowledge and create conditions based on this fact, conditions for teachers to work collectively and collaboratively and openly, or we create conditions that encourage resistance, secrecy, and sabotage."[11]

2. "Team-Driven" Professional Development

In almost every successful business or nonprofit organization one can find today, people work in teams—except in education. The reason teamwork is now the norm in most workplaces is simple: teams generally find far better solutions to problems than do individuals who try to solve them alone. Educators arguably face problems at least as difficult as those found in other workplaces, but—as we learned from the description above—the way in which educators work and the very structure of their day do not allow for collaboration.

Nor do teachers receive useful feedback from supervisors. Typically, the only "supervision" a teacher receives is perhaps a fifteen-minute visit from the principal or assistant principal of the school once a year. The purpose of the visit is so that the principal can fill out the requisite teacher evaluation form—usually a one-page checklist. At its best, this system is a means to weed out the worst performing teachers, but in fact, union contracts and leader timidity combine in most places to ensure that few teachers ever get an unsatisfactory rating—let alone fired.

In most schools today, there is no system for improving teaching. Teachers struggling with issues—everything from how to reach a particular student to how to meet the new subject content standards—rarely have anyone to whom they can turn for help. The overwhelming majority of public school teachers must work—and struggle—alone.

From the beginning, Central Park East was organized around a team structure, and Meier and her colleagues created a schedule that would allow time for teachers to collaborate. Teams of three to five teachers have responsibility for the same seventy-five to eighty students for two years, and they meet for several hours each week to plan lessons together and to discuss individual student needs and progress. While this structure is an essential way to ensure that students do not fall through the cracks, it is also an opportunity for teachers to create greater subject content integration and coherence through team planning. Finally, it is a form of professional development. Colleagues have time to question one another and to learn from each other.

A core tenet of the Central Park East philosophy is that the best professional development comes from this kind of peer "supervision" and ongoing professional dialogue. CPESS teachers weren't just organized into grade-level teams. The entire faculty, in fact, operated as a team. The size of the school was determined, in part, by Meier's insistence that all of the teachers in the school had to fit into a normal-sized classroom so that talking together would be the way in which they conducted their business. Meier explains:

> This continuing dialogue, face to face, over and over, is a powerful educative force. It is our primary form of staff development. When people ask me how we "train" new teachers, I say that the school itself is an educator for the kids and staff, it's its own staff development project. The habits of mind, our

five essential questions, and the habits of work we encourage in our students are thus exemplified in the daily life of the staff. We too weigh evidence, explore alternative viewpoints, conjecture about other possibilities, make connections, and ask, So what? We too must meet deadlines and keep our word and communicate clearly.[12]

In summary, the vast majority of teachers are not motivated to continuously improve their teaching with a once a year drop-in visit from the principal. Nor is the occasional drop-in professional development program of any real value. Teachers improve in their work through contact with highly effective peers and continuous dialogue and inquiry. Peer supervision is ultimately the most effective form of accountability in education—indeed, as it is in most other professions.

3. "Localized" Authority

Such an "accountability system" only works when teachers have the collective authority to make changes, however. In most public schools today, we have the worst of two worlds. Teachers now have much more visible responsibility and accountability for improving test scores, but almost no authority. What can they change? Not their working conditions—the numbers of students they see in a day or the lack of opportunities to work with and learn from colleagues. Not the school and district practices that get in the way of involving parents, like the ones described earlier. Not even, in the vast majority of cases, the "professional development" program or the curriculum and books chosen.

If one feels one cannot change the circumstances that substantially determine the "product" of one's work, what, then, is the incentive to try something new in the classroom?

Back in the late 1980s, CPESS negotiated what are called "waivers" from many state and district regulations, which permitted them a far higher degree of control over the school than most public schools had. At its inception, the professional authority was "localized" at Central Park East. Groups of teachers determined the graduation requirements, the structure of the school day and curriculum, the most effective ways of supporting student learning, and the ways in which they, as adults, would work and learn together. They also made all the hiring decisions.

With the new wave of accountability requirements, these waivers have become much harder to secure, which means that most schools—including Central Park East—have less authority today. This has serious implications both for the school and for the kind of person who is likely to be attracted to teaching.

I believe that because of the autonomy the school was given, Central Park East attracted and supported a new breed of teacher—an educator-entrepreneur. It attracted individuals who were excited at the prospect of creating not just a better curriculum, but also a better way of educating all children. It was an opportunity to do what I call "educational research and development." This spirit must be encouraged if we are to redesign the American system of public education.

4. A Culture of "Face-to-Face" and "Data-Driven"Accountability

Nothing I have written is meant to imply that educators should not be held accountable. What I am saying, simply, is that teachers are more motivated to improve their practice when they are given more responsibility for decision making, along with accountability. In business, leaders talk about the people "closest to the problem" being the most qualified to find better solutions. Why doesn't this same principle apply in education?

Teachers at CPESS had more responsibility, but also more accountability—especially of the most visible kinds. First, the very nature of their graduation expectations—requiring all students to exhibit mastery in fourteen specific areas—routinely put the products of both student and teacher work up for public display. Remember that outsiders were a part of every panel that examined student work and determined whether an individual was ready to graduate. The school also regularly invited teams of outsiders—colleagues from other schools, college professors, and business and community representatives—to audit student portfolios. CPESS teachers wanted to know how their students' work stacked up against adults' expectations in a wide variety of circumstances. CPESS was a member of the Coalition of Essential Schools and often had hundreds of visitors in their school each week. They also took part in a number of different kinds of School Quality Reviews with other Coalition schools.

Finally, all CPESS students were required to take—and to pass—New York state basic competency tests in writing and math. Teachers met this testing requirement, but they were much less successful at improving scores on other kinds of tests for reasons that deserve some discussion.

These days, "data-driven" reform and accountability are the mantras of many superintendents and policy makers. But what these mean in practice are highly problematic for students and teachers. Typically, the only data that ever gets discussed in districts and in the media are the scores on standardized tests. However, the Central Park East story suggests that other kinds of data can often tell us much more about teacher effectiveness and school quality.

SAT scores and scores from other such tests were of concern to CPESS teachers because of the extent to which they are used as "gate-keeping devices" for students wanting to go to college. And they were a source of profound frustration. CPESS had eleventh- and twelfth-grade students succeeding in college math courses that normally required passing a standardized math exam in order to register—an exam that some of their students would not have passed if they had been required to take it. Over time, CPESS worked with admissions officers in a number of colleges to help them find other ways of determining a student's readiness for college-level work.

CPESS and many other small high schools are extraordinarily successful when measured by a wide range of quantitative indicators: they have significantly fewer discipline problems; higher daily attendance and graduation rates; higher rates of teacher, student, and parent satisfaction; and nearly 100 percent college attendance—to name a few.[13] But despite their best efforts, teachers did not see a significant improvement in students' standardized test scores at CPESS.

The problem is that most standardized tests in use today, including SATs, favor students from more middle-class backgrounds. As much as anything, they test whether or not children were sent to a quality preschool, how many books were in the house when students were growing up, how many times children were taken to museums and other interesting places, and so on. For these reasons, a growing number of highly selective colleges no longer require students to submit SAT scores and weigh other kinds of information in admissions decisions.

In a recent speech Meier said, "We can change students' lives more quickly than we can change students' test scores."[14] She went on to suggest that the most important data a school might collect were the results of longitudinal studies of graduates. CPESS faculty, in fact, collected this and other data and considered all of it on a regular basis in order to determine how they might improve the school. According to Meier:

> The staff spends all year reviewing its fourteen graduation requirements, and each fall comes up with new versions of one or another of them. The experience of our alumni/ae, of external visitors, the work of our colleagues across the nation as well as our own daily practice, all lead to such revisions. At various steps along the way the latest drafts are circulated and debated by students and teachers. We added a new section of computer literacy after considerable debate about whether it should be part of all our requirements or a separate one. Recently we added an emphasis on experimental science and redrafted the math requirements to better reflect the latest national Council of Teachers of Math (NCTM) standards. . . . Similarly, issues of

behavior, school management, and student/teacher relations occupy our attention.[15]

New forms of both data-driven and face-to-face accountability are important as a means of ensuring quality and continuous improvement. In CPESS and other New Village Schools, there is simply no way for either students or teachers to hide mediocre performance. Accountability is highly public, every day—but only if the school is small enough.

In an essay that argues powerfully for small schools (an issue to which we turn in a moment), Meier writes, "Only in a small school can teachers know who talks well but doesn't teach well, and vice versa. They know who is late, who is unprepared, and who in quiet and yet unexpected ways comes through for their kids and colleagues, goes the extra mile. They also can begin the difficult task of being as critical of each other as they are accustomed to being of their students, respecting their colleagues enough to ask hard questions of each other."[16]

In summary, we have looked at a number of key design elements in one prototype New Village School—Central Park East—that positively influence both student and teacher motivation to do quality work. Each of these elements is both critical and very rare in most schools today. But there is a foundation on which these design elements are built that remains to be explored. For most of these design elements to work, New Village Schools must be small, and both students and teachers must choose to be there. And so school size and choice are the issues to which we now turn.

WHY SCHOOL SIZE MATTERS

The issue of school size has gotten some attention recently in the media—in part because of the substantial grants recently given by the Bill & Melinda Gates Foundation to create many more new small high schools around the country. The foundation's grant making has been influenced by the growing body of evidence that it is not possible to substantially improve teacher and student motivation and performance in large, anonymous schools. There is now more than a decade of research that points to the benefits of smaller schools.[17] But creating smaller schools is not a new idea, and it is not a panacea.

Educators in independent schools have understood the benefits of smallness for a long time. Consider the size of the typical elite private day school. It is very hard to find one with more than a hundred students in a grade, or four hundred students in a high school. Many of these schools have ten applicants for every position and opportunities to raise substantial amounts of money for new facilities, but they choose not to expand.

And new public charter schools in America enroll only about 250 students on average. These schools are not usually required to heed the "economies of scale and efficiency" arguments made by school planners—bigger is cheaper—and so they, too, have made a conscious choice to keep their schools small. Why?

These educators know something about the importance of scale or size in creating a school where all students and teachers are motivated to work hard and continue to learn. People—students and teachers alike—can hide or get lost in big schools. It's much harder to hide in a smaller place where, as Meier said, everyone knows who comes in late and who is prepared. Smaller schools encourage the kind of face-to-face accountability I have been describing. Such visibility provides a subtle but effective form of peer pressure.

Compliance versus Commitment

In my experience, large schools and districts (and most other bureaucracies) are almost universally organized around a set of norms and behaviors all having to do with *compliance*. Students have to comply with teacher rules and demands, teachers have to comply with the expectations of the principal, and the school principals must comply with district mandates. Relationships among most people are determined by roles. There is little or no interpersonal loyalty. And so most people in such organizations tend to do only the minimum to get by—whether they are students, teachers, or principals. Many survive by creating small, informal networks of friends and colleagues that become a kind of community and an island of humanity in a sea of indifference.

By contrast, effective small schools succeed because they create a culture of *commitment*. The loyalty most students and teachers feel is not just to a small network of buddies, but also to a larger entity—to the *school community*. Norms of behavior for both adults and students are established collaboratively and maintained less through formal rules than through the loyalty individuals feel to their shared community.

One can see this loyalty in both small and big things at Central Park East and in many other similar small schools. There is no graffiti on the walls in these schools and very little trash on the floors not because there's a rule, but because students care. Teachers are available to help students after school and work long hours not because a contract requires them to—it doesn't—but because they care. Caring, commitment, and collaboration, rather than compliance, are the qualities of culture in good small schools. The motivations to work hard are thus rooted in relationships, not rules—a theme we will explore further in the last chapter.

This culture extends to the parents as well. Rather than being seen as adversaries or "slackers"—which is how they're treated in most large schools—parents are considered to be a part of the community. Indeed, many parents of students attending private and public charter schools give "belonging to a community" as the main reason for choosing a particular school for their children.

But What about "Efficiency"?

Skeptics of small schools tend to worry about two things—increased costs per student and the need to build new small school buildings. Both are legitimate questions—for which there are some surprising answers.

Small public high schools are given the same amount of money per student as the large comprehensive high schools. They are, in fact, no more expensive to operate on a daily basis. Because these schools are given their per student allocation in one lump sum, though, they can make their own independent budgetary decisions. As we have seen, most of these schools use their resources very differently. Students do not have a choice of four hundred courses or three sports each season. Believing that academics come first, CPESS did not have large numbers of expensive varsity teams, though most students were involved in before- and after-school sports programs. Many of these schools also raise funds from private sources aggressively. This outside money is used to pay for summer or Saturday academic "catch-up" programs needed by many students. It is also used to pay for the increased amount of time these schools spend on faculty professional development.

Even when factoring in these supplemental funds that small schools may depend on, they still significantly outperform large schools on another indicator of efficiency. When one analyzes these schools, *in terms of costs per graduating student*, they are significantly less expensive, according to a recent study done by Norm Fructer and his colleagues at The Institute for Education and Social Policy.[18] As we've seen, Central Park East graduates about 95 percent of its students for a fractionally higher total cost per student than most New York City high schools that graduate only 50 percent or fewer of their students.

The new school building programs in most states are another serious example of faulty accounting. First, states are still building enormous schools, despite more than a decade of research on the benefits of small school size. Second, most states require new schools to have certain facilities, which are very costly and which may or may not be appropriate for a small school: a library and gym of a certain size, classrooms of a particular dimension, and so on. None of these regulations take into consideration the ways in which small schools use community resources and physical space very differently.

Fortunately, the creation of small schools does not depend on new school construction. In New York City and elsewhere, there are numerous examples of distinctly different small schools sharing the same large school physical plant or operating successfully in other kinds of buildings. Today in New York City, there are at least a hundred new small high schools that have been created in the last decade, which serve about sixty thousand students. Most all of them coexist with other schools, cultural and community institutions, or businesses.

A High School Transformation

The Julia Richman story is one of the most dramatic and successful examples of new use of a school building. Located in New York City, Julia Richman was one of the worst-performing high schools in the early 1990s. Only about two-thirds of the students showed up on any given day—perhaps because most knew there was no point. The graduation rate from Julia Richman was 37 percent. The school had been on the city's list of lowest-performing schools for twenty years. Seemingly, everything had been tried, and nothing had worked.[19]

Deborah Meier and Marcia Brevot, with the support of colleagues from six other small schools in New York City, proposed a radical solution to the reorganization of Julia Richman and one other high school in the Bronx, and city school officials agreed. In 1993, instead of admitting six hundred new ninth-graders, the students went to six new small high schools that had been established in leased space in different parts of the city. The following year, these new high schools each had two hundred ninth- and tenth-graders, who would have gone to Julia Richman. This process continued for the next two years until the last class graduated from Julia Richman in 1997.

The now-empty building was refurbished, and two of the new small high schools that had been created moved back in, along with two other new small high schools. (By then the other four newly created high schools serving Julia Richman students had found space where they preferred to remain.) But the project's leaders wanted the building to be a different kind of learning community, and so they also invited a K–8 school, a middle school for autistic children, an infant-toddler center and daycare program, a student health services center, and a teacher resource center to share the space with them.

Today, the renamed Julia Richman Education Complex is a compelling monument to the possibilities of school reinvention. One can walk down the hall from a high school to a fourth-grade classroom, and in fact, many of the students in the four high school programs in the building do community service in the K–8 school. There are no physical walls separating the program spaces, but each has its own identity, and the building—once in the worst shape of any high school in the city—is immaculate. Common spaces like the auditorium, cafeteria, and gym are shared—and the high schools even field a couple of shared varsity sports teams. A council of principals and teachers, representing all the programs, governs the building.

The successful Julia Richman effort lent energy and credibility to the creation of dozens of new small high schools during the mid-1990s. A number of New York nonprofit organizations—including New Visions for New Public Schools, the Center for Collaborative Education, and Acorn—have given vital assistance in helping to establish these schools. And in December 2000 the Bill & Melinda Gates Foundation teamed with the Carnegie Foundation and the Open Society Institute to donate $30 million to create fifty or more additional new and converted high schools like Julia Richman in New York City.

But the greatest difference is in the lives of the students who attend the school today. In many cases, they are the younger brothers and sisters of the students who attended the old Julia Richman, but their experience of school—their sense of hope and possibilities for the future—has been transformed. Each of the four small high schools in the building has a distinctive program and identity, but all share about a 95 percent graduation rate and more than a 90 percent college attendance rate.

Smaller Schools: Necessary but Not Sufficient

The data are overwhelming: smaller schools significantly outperform larger schools with comparable student populations on nearly every indicator of "effectiveness." But smaller school size is not a silver bullet. It is a necessary—but not sufficient—condition for the creation of a higher-performing New Village School. The great danger is that the creation of smaller public schools will become the latest education fad that fails unless educators pay careful attention to all of the other ingredients for success described in this chapter. The most important element of success in small schools is a set of beliefs about what constitutes powerful teaching and learning. The attributes of effective teaching and learning are well summarized as a part of the current education proposal guidelines of the Bill & Melinda Gates Foundation. They are listed on the foundation's website and are as follows:[20]

Teachers Focused on Improving Teaching and Learning

The Foundation's education grant programs are predicated on three essential components of powerful teaching and learning (adapted from *How People Learn: Bridging Research and Practice*, National Research Council, 1999) in a standards-based technology-enabled environment:

- *Active Inquiry*: Students are engaged in active participation, exploration, and research; activities draw out perceptions and develop understanding; students are encouraged to make decisions about their learning; and teachers utilize the diverse experiences of students to build effective learning experiences.

- *In-Depth Learning*: The focus is competence, not coverage. Students struggle with complex problems, explore core concepts to develop deep understanding, and apply knowledge in real-world contexts.

- *Performance Assessment:* Clear expectations define what students should know and be able to do; students produce quality work products and present to real audiences; student work shows evidence of understanding, not just recall; assessment tasks allow students to exhibit higher-order thinking; and teachers and students set learning goals and monitor progress.

In summary, smaller schools create the possibility for very different kinds of relationships both among adults and between adults and students—relationships that can significantly improve motivations for learning and accountability for results. But these efforts must be grounded in a clear understanding of what constitutes powerful teaching and learning and in a commitment to continuous critical dialogue for improvement. Without this clear commitment to intellectual rigor, the great danger of small schools is that they can become a little more than a mutual admiration society.

WHAT ABOUT TECHNOLOGY?

The other education fad or "silver bullet" that has the potential for being abused in school improvement efforts is the use of new technologies. Similar to the innovations that small schools represent, it is easy to see the many advantages of exciting new technologies applied to education and thus to lose focus in improving teaching and learning and building community.

Technology, used well, is a powerful learning tool. The Internet allows students to do more original research, using primary sources. Distance learning enables schools to provide Advanced Placement or other specialized courses that they would not otherwise have the faculty to offer. Computers enable students to explore alternative solutions to scientific and mathematical problems with ease—to explore "what-if" questions in ways that would not otherwise be possible. They make the creation of sophisticated presentations and revision of writing comparatively easy. Computers are also a very powerful tool for diagnosing students' specific strengths and weaknesses in subject areas and for individualizing learning. Digital portfolios, created and stored on computers, offer the opportunity of allowing many people to view, compare, and critique student work. Finally, technology can greatly enhance information sharing and communication and so help to build community.

But for every exciting application of new technologies in education, I have seen others that merely add seductive window dressing to bad teaching. The most common use of computers in schools is to play games or to jazz up assignments that have no educational value. I once visited a "school of the future" where every eighth-grade student had his or her own laptop. As I went from desk to desk, students eagerly showed off their latest effort—a second grade–level presentation about their life history, complete with music and animation. No doubt, creating the work had been entertaining, but I saw no evidence of learning from the assignment. Technology can also as readily undermine community as build it. I have been in schools and districts where every teacher has been given e-mail access—and wished they hadn't. The number of mean-spirited e-mails being sent with impunity was demoralizing the entire staff and greatly outweighed any possible benefit from increased communication.

As I write this book, former secretary of education William Bennett has teamed up with former junk bond dealer Michael Milken to create an online K–12 school. Their professed aim, besides making a profit, is to offer more choices to families—especially the growing numbers who now choose to home school their children. They hope to have fifty thousand children enrolled by 2004.[21] While I think choice of education programs is important and a topic we will soon explore further and I agree that having online courses available for students can be a valuable addition to their learning, going to school online is something entirely different.

A wise former teacher and mentor of mine, Joseph Featherstone, once defined good teaching as "the art of creating the context for a thoughtful conversation." In learning, there is simply no substitute for dialogue that provokes questions, analysis, and reflection. Home-schooled students often do well because they have more opportunities for this kind of dialogue at home in a more respectful environment than would be possible in their public schools. This need for thoughtful dialogue is why learning is, and has always been, a profoundly social activity that develops both IQ and EQ. Online communication with a teacher one has never met—much like an online "friend"—is, at best, a supplement and not a substitute for the real thing.

One Kind Doesn't Fit All

While I have used Central Park East Secondary School as a model for analyzing the essential elements of what I call the New Village School, in fact, many hundreds of very different public New Village Schools have been started in the last decade. They share most—if not all—of the elements described in this chapter, but they are very much tailored to the needs and interests of the community of teachers and families they serve. I include here a brief description of several interesting models so that readers can get a sense of the diversity of these schools.

The Minnesota New Country School

The Minnesota New Country School is located in Henderson, Minnesota, a rural farming community sixty miles southwest of Minneapolis. It is a charter school that serves seventh- to twelfth-graders from a ten-district area. The school has no courses or classes. Instead, students complete individual and group projects in order to show mastery of a series of competencies that are required for graduation—much like the Chugach example. The staff acts as facilitators, helping students with technology, community resources, and postsecondary institutions. The school is entirely managed by teachers, who have formed the only public school teacher cooperative in the nation.

The Met

The Met is a public high school located in Providence, Rhode Island. The majority of its students have dropped out or been expelled from their local public school. Students spend most of their week with an adult mentor in work-based internships of their choice—both nonprofit and for profit. Met teachers, students, mentors, and family members work together to create personalized learning plans for each student and use comprehensive, performance-based assessment tools to measure students' achievement. In June 2000, the Met had its first graduation. Every student applied and was accepted to a postsecondary institution.

High Tech High

High Tech High is a new charter high school in San Diego. Innovative features of the educational program include a project-based curriculum, tight linkages to the high-tech workplace, student understanding and use of information technology, strong and varied adult relationships (with advisors at the school and industry mentors), and seminars. Students from diverse backgrounds and differing skill levels work together in small groups. The school facility design offers expansive student workstation and project space to encourage both collaborative learning and individual exploration and gives each student solo access to a computer for half of each day.

Francis Parker

The Francis Parker Charter School serves 360 students in grades 7–12 from more than thirty suburban communities in north central Massachusetts. The school's philosophy is based upon the Ten Common Principles of The Coalition of Essential Schools, where the goal of education is to teach all students to use their minds well. This means developing intellectual skills in a few essential areas, such as writing, reading, and mathematics, through exploration of "essential questions" that cross disciplinary lines. Students must complete various demonstrations of mastery and portfolio require-ments in order to move from one school division to the next, as well as to graduate.

While located in very diverse communities and serving quite different students, all of these schools nonetheless share the qualities we've discussed in this chapter that are most important to student and teacher motivation. Each of them (and a small number of schools like them) has been given a grant by the Bill & Melinda Gates Foundation to help others who are inter-ested in starting similar kinds of schools. Finally, they are also all schools of choice. Both teachers and families are associated with the school because they choose to be—an issue to which we now turn.

THE PROMISE AND PERILS OF SCHOOL CHOICE

In addition to the elements of successful New Village Schools already described in this chapter, all of the schools mentioned above share one other characteristic that fundamentally affects student and teacher motiva-tion: choice. Both teachers and families choose to be associated with these schools, and I believe this choice is a key component of their success—but not necessarily for the reasons given by many choice proponents.

Choice As a "Market Incentive"

The most common argument in favor of school choice today is made by those who want to "deregulate" education. The theory was first popularized in the book *Politics, Markets, and America's Schools*. Authors John Chubb and Terry Moe argued that the most efficient way to reform American public education is to create a free market, where parents can choose the school they wish to send their child to—with a government-provided voucher or subsidy. The theory is that, in a market environment, the most successful schools would flourish, while schools less frequently chosen would end up going out of business.

Since the publication of the book, the arguments both in favor of and against school choice have grown—as have the opportunities for more Americans to choose different kinds of public schools through the rapid growth of the charter school movement. While the enabling legislation—and thus the schools themselves—varies greatly from state to state, generally charter schools are publicly funded schools, which are organized and managed outside the confines of the public school district bureaucracy. Students and their families "choose" to go to these schools, and the state or district provides per student funding to the charter school usually comparable to what other public schools receive in conventional districts.

Minnesota was the first state to pass charter school legislation in 1991. As of January 2000, thirty-six states and the District of Columbia had charter school legislation, and there were more than sixteen hundred charter school sites in operation, serving about 250,000 students or about 0.8 percent of the total public school population.[22] By December 2000, there were an additional five hundred or so charter schools.

Despite this rapid growth, most school districts have paid charter schools comparatively little attention as potential competitors. They know, I think, that the chances of a public school actually being closed due to "market forces" are remote, at best, unless we move to the kind of licensing system discussed earlier. They may also observe that, in fact, new school start-ups face the same obstacles as new businesses. The requisite leadership and financial backing are hard to come by in both cases.

What seems clear, then, is that without a conscious decision to move to a system that allows school choice for all families, the "market forces" strategy will have a marginal impact on our existing public education system, at best. But my deeper concern is that the highly charged debates about the merits of vouchers and the marketplace in education obscure the most important *educational* reasons for school choice.

School Choice As a Reflection of Student Differences

The reason why "one size doesn't fit all" in schools is because students and their families vary greatly in their interests, needs, and—most important— the ways that children learn. Howard Gardner's theory of "multiple intelligences"—made popular in his famous book *Frames of Mind*—is now widely accepted in education. At last we have a theory that helps explain what many good educators have long known: while all students learn through active engagement, individual children have distinctively different kinds of intelligence (or what some call "learning styles") and so approach learning in fundamentally different ways.

When learning to read, for example, some children benefit most from what is called a "phonics" approach, where they are taught how to sound out or decode individual words and parts of words. But other children's reading can be hindered with this approach because they respond best to the challenge of learning the sounds and meanings of whole words in the context of a good story (an approach called "whole language"). Good teachers often blend the two approaches and adapt their teaching strategies to individual needs.

But it is not just a teaching strategy that must be adaptive to different student learning styles. My experience is that, especially as children become adolescents, their learning interests and needs become highly differentiated. Equally but differently gifted, my own three children are a case in point. One child needed a more highly structured learning environment, while the other two thrived in an environment that allowed for more self-direction.

We have freedom of choice of religion in our society. Why not in public education? One brand does not work for everyone in either case. Why give a choice of schools only to those who can afford it? An educationally compelling reason for school choice, then, is to create a greater diversity of public schools that are more reflective of the different needs, interests, and values of students and their families.

Choice As Precondition for Community

Perhaps the most compelling educational argument for school choice, though, is the one least frequently mentioned: it is a necessary precondition for the creation of a highly motivated learning community.

Earlier in this chapter, I described the essential differences between a school culture that is a rule-driven, compliance-based bureaucracy versus a relationship-driven, commitment-based community. The difference in the quality of the motivation to work hard and to succeed for both adults and students is simply night and day and is a topic I will explore further in the next chapter.

But in order to create meaningful community, everyone that is a part of such an endeavor must feel that they want to be there, that the choice is theirs and freely made. If they are forced to be a part of a school community, then the bond of and loyalty to the relationships that are the core motivator to work harder breaks down or is never developed. This is not to say that every student who starts out at a New Village School must already be excited to be there and highly motivated. It takes time for students to become acculturated into a school community and to develop relationships and loyalties to both peers and adults.

Nevertheless, the act of choosing is the first step down a very different path—*even if the choice to be made is more apparent than real*. Ann Cook is principal of the Urban Academy in New York, a highly successful alternative high school where many of the students have been expelled from other high schools are so are assigned to this school as a "last chance." Even though most students are required to attend her school by the district bureaucracy, Ann insists that all perspective students spend a day visiting and interviewing before they are "accepted." She understands that the act of choosing the school—and of feeling chosen by the school—is critical in the development of students' desire to refashion their lives and to achieve.

The Pitfalls of Choice

While being able to choose one's school is very important for the educational reasons cited, it is also a public policy that carries real risks that are seldom mentioned by proponents. Creating genuine choice of public schools may lead to greater racial and religious separatism and inequality of educational opportunities. School choice is simultaneously a profoundly democratic value and potentially a very real threat to democracy.

The enormous variety among the new public charter schools that have been created in the last ten years speaks to the desire of racial and religious minorities, as well as individuals with particular interests, to create schools that are more reflective of their distinct cultures and values. There are so-called Afro-centric charter schools and fundamentalist charter schools, schools that emphasize the arts, and those that focus on science and engineering.

The profound differences among these schools challenges a basic tenet of public education. In America, we have long believed that we need "common" public schools in order to learn how to get along together in a democracy. But is this really true?

Will the existence of these schools—with their pronounced differences—encourage greater divisiveness and/or misunderstanding among different groups in our society over time? While we are not yet sure, at the least, this greater diversity of schools underscores the need for some common national educational standards for citizenship, and I suggested an approach for embedding some citizenship competencies in a national literacy test in chapter 4. But in the final analysis, I am not worried about differences in school cultures leading to greater ethnic and religious intolerance in our society. In fact, I think the opposite may happen. I base this hope on two very different kinds of school experiences and observations.

As a classroom teacher, I eventually learned that the opportunities for individual choice and self-expression I offered in assignments and the more I encouraged students to share their individuality through their work, the greater the sense of collaboration and community in the classroom. It is a fascinating paradox that proved itself over and over to me in every class I taught. Students were more ready to appreciate one another and to work together when they felt their individual identities were strong and respected. Jean Piaget made the same observation in his research: greater individuation leads to greater collaboration.

I made my second observations as a senior researcher for the National Study of Charter Schools in a study funded by the U.S. Department of Education. As we explored the fascinating diversity of charter schools that were being established in the late 1990s, I was most struck by the fact that one of the common traits of virtually every charter school we studied was the emphasis on values. More striking still was the fact that all of these schools taught the importance of respect as a fundamental value. I have found that the same emphasis on respect as a basic democratic value emerges in virtually every community-based discussion of what should be taught in schools.

America is truly—and increasingly—a rainbow rather than a melting pot. Despite—or perhaps because of—our vast cultural, ethnic, and religious differences, the overwhelming majority of Americans want children to learn the importance of respect for others and tolerance of differences. Allowing public schools to fashion their own distinct identity may actually lead to a greater emphasis on these values than what we find in our existing, "melting pot" public schools today, where differences are papered over and rarely discussed.

The danger that greater school choice will increase, rather than reduce, educational inequities is the other great risk in this policy. And I think it is a very real one, indeed. In the second edition of my book *How Schools Change*, I described how, in one Cambridge, Massachusetts, high school, choice of programs led to increased inequities in the levels of student achievement between different programs. And a recent report on the results of school choice in New Zealand, *When Schools Compete: A Cautionary Tale* by Edward B. Fiske and Helen F. Ladd, underscored the growing disparity of achievement levels among different schools in a country where everyone chooses their child's school.

Many advocates of school choice continue to struggle with this problem, and so do I. There are some obvious remedies in the form of both sticks and carrots. A licensing system, such as Paul Hill proposed, that would close down underperforming schools would serve as a powerful regulatory function. Indeed, ensuring quality choices for all students would be the first and most important task of school boards and the state. And a government policy that created adequate funding for all schools (a problem we will discuss in the next chapter) and that offered additional money to schools that accepted at-risk students would provide assistance and incentives to better serve this population. But these policies are still essentially in the "research and development" phase and have yet to be tested on a large scale.

The dangers of a school choice policy are quite real, and as we move more toward a choice-based system of education, we will need both new policies and careful monitoring. When it comes to reinventing public schools, there is no simple panacea. There are also risks in many of the education changes I have advocated throughout this book. We must acknowledge these. But the risks inherent in trying to patch up our assembly-line school system through the simple-minded strategy of high-stakes testing, I believe, are greater by far. Large numbers of children are suffering from the effects of schooling that is mediocre or worse. This does not have to be so.

5

WHAT MUST LEADERS DO?

IN the past decade or so, "leadership" has become quite the buzzword. Everyone seems to agree that we need more of it at every level. In education, many now believe we have a "leadership crisis." In fact, several of the large national foundations have recently initiated new grant-making programs aimed at improving educational leadership.

However, rarely do I hear much discussion of what we really mean by leadership in education or even what we most need leaders to do. In this chapter, I will first outline what I think are some urgent priorities for political and business leaders related to education. Then I will explore a new model for the kind of educational leadership most needed today.

THE POLITICAL LEADERSHIP WE NEED

It is time for politicians to acknowledge that the high-stakes tests strategy, like every other effort to regulate public education in the past, is not getting the desired results. The state tests do not assess the skills most needed by students today, for the most part, and they are increasing the high school dropout rate, especially among minorities. They are also fermenting greater divisiveness within communities and contributing to the demoralization of teachers and students.

My experience is that most politicians don't even have an elementary understanding of the education problems we face; yet they are trying to unilaterally impose solutions on educators. They would never treat business leaders and their problems that way. They would discuss the issues and problem solve together. Why should educators be treated as second-class citizens?

What politicians must realize is that fear is not the best motivator for change. Increasing the pressure on teachers or students, or both, will not substantially improve the system. The new state tests do not create the kinds of positive incentives or *motivations* needed for education reinvention. They do not encourage the creation of the more collaborative and collegial *relationships* needed to work effectively for change. Nor do they alter the *conditions* that inhibit effective teaching and learning. And they do not contribute to the development of the *capacities* of educators to tackle a set of new, and far more difficult, educational challenges. (We'll discuss these critical elements later in this chapter.)

State politicians would argue that it is the job of school district leaders to create new educational structures and develop educators' capacities. But most of them are also prisoners of an overregulated, compliance-based system that is incapable of reinventing itself.

The only way we are going to significantly raise all students' levels of competence is by creating entirely new education systems, with different incentives and accountability measures that enhance both student and teacher motivation, improve teaching conditions, create new relationships, and develop educators' capacities. Politicians don't know how to do that by themselves. They must involve educators in the process. Essentially, we must decrease, rather than increase, the state regulation of education and develop new accountability systems with educators—instead of imposing them unilaterally. Politicians must help the public understand that anything less will fail.

Creating a More Flexible Regulatory System for Education

In chapter 3, I outlined elements of a new regulatory system for education that would create much stronger incentives for educational "research and development" and improved student and teacher performance. They are summarized below.

1. School Boards License Individuals or Groups to Run Schools

The "unit of improvement" in education is not the school district. It is the individual school. Districts don't teach students—schools do. Most school board members and district-level leaders don't know what good teaching looks like or even the conditions needed to create good teaching and learning. In rare cases—especially in smaller districts—they can learn. But it is probably easier and more efficient for school boards to reconceptualize their role as essentially licensing authorities, as suggested by Paul Hill. Let school boards grant five-year licenses to individuals or groups wanting to run schools. Licenses would be renewable only if state-supervised School Quality Reviews indicated that schools were successful.

2. The State Supervises School Quality Reviews and Licenses Academic Standards and Teachers

Bad schools can hide behind good test scores, and good schools don't necessarily have the best test results. The money now spent by states on developing and administering standardized tests would be better spent on a system of School Quality Reviews, such as Rhode Island has done. Both educators and the general public will learn more from the results of peer reviews of schools that take into consideration a range of indices of an effective school. This system of School Quality Reviews would also ensure that school boards are doing an effective job of granting licenses to run schools only to qualified individuals and groups.

There is not just one definition of "academic rigor" or a common agreement on what students most need to know and be able to do, and so states should not impose one set of academic standards on all students. Rather, they should license different systems of academic standards for use in the state's public schools. Everything from standards based on the Coalition of Essential Schools' ten common principles to E. D. Hirsch's cultural literacy framework could be licensed. State-level peer and community review of standards can ensure that various standards systems have coherency, rigor, and effective methods of assessment. The state of Georgia has recently developed a system similar to the one I'm proposing to license early childhood education programs and has found it to be a very effective system for allowing competing providers.

States have traditionally licensed educators, but the skills required are often minimal, and they are assessed with a multiple-choice test that does not access actual teaching skills. The license is also renewed too easily—usually by taking a few courses. Both aspects of the system must be changed.

It should be relatively easy to get an initial or "apprentice" teaching license—enabling many to try out the profession without having to take numerous—and often useless—education courses. But teachers should be required to submit evidence of teaching and subject content proficiency after a few years in order to gain a "journeyman's" license—through submission of teacher portfolios with sample lessons, student work, and videotapes of teaching.

The National Board for Professional Teaching Standards has already developed such a system, and it has proven remarkably successful as a means of assessing teacher quality. I would add another level to the National Board's and states' certification programs, however. With documented evidence of skills in supervision and/or curriculum development, an educator could be promoted to the level of "master" teacher—thus providing a career ladder in education that does not now exist.

A system similar to this has been proposed by Alan Odden, an education researcher at the University of Wisconsin, and is being tested by the Cincinnati Public Schools. But I would make one important addition in order to deal with the tenure problem. I would require that licenses to teach be renewed every five or so years and that the criteria for renewal be the same as for initial licensing—proficiency-based assessment of teacher competence. If states adopted such a requirement, union-district agreements granting teachers lifetime jobs would be superseded. The state law would be that no one teaches without a license.

3. The Federal Government Supervises Literacy and Numeracy Testing and Ensures Adequate and Equitable Funding for Education

Why do we need fifty poor quality state tests when we already have one decent national set of tests? The federal government has sponsored the NAEP since the early 1970s. The reading and writing tests developed by NAEP have been in use much longer and are more highly regarded than most comparable state tests. This system could be made more performance-based and expanded to gather comparative data on every school in the country. It could also be given online and used as a diagnostic tool to do ongoing assessments of students' strengths and weaknesses.

An expanded NAEP testing program should be confined to literacy and numeracy measures only—with the literacy test having a strong civics component. Other subject areas such as science and social studies are so controversial or content-driven that a national test is both unrealistic and undesirable. A national testing program should not lead to the creation of a set of national standards or a national curriculum.

I believe the federal government must also play a role in creating more adequate and equitable funding mechanisms for schools. Why should education budgets be based on local property taxes, as they are in most states, or be a prisoner of voter approval for new tax levies every year or two? Some states like Vermont have created much more equitable funding formulas for all schools, but the federal government needs to equalize education funding between the richer and poor states—and direct additional resources to schools that serve the most at-risk students.

The policy framework I've outlined is neither entirely new nor untested. Each of these recommendations is based on a practice that has already proven successful in some form. I've also discussed these ideas with leading educators and policy makers. All agree that these proposals are ambitious—even visionary—but no one has told me that they cannot or should not be done.

However, the set of policy recommendations above is not a buffet from which items can be randomly chosen or discarded. Rather, it represents an effort to conceptualize an entirely new system, which is meant to replace the existing dysfunctional accountability system in its entirety. While others may devise a different architecture, I am sure that what is needed is an entirely new design. I do not think partial efforts or a mix of old and new accountability systems—such as having both high-stakes state tests and state-sponsored school quality reviews—will be effective ultimately.

Politicians and educators, working alone, cannot make the sweeping kinds of changes proposed here. To develop public acceptance for a differently regulated education system, we need new forms of leadership from the business community as well.

THE BUSINESS LEADERSHIP WE NEED

As I've said, for the past fifteen years or so education reform efforts in this country have been "business driven." Business leaders have played a vital role in helping political and educational leaders to understand that all students need new skills and significantly higher levels of competency in order to succeed in today's knowledge economy and rapidly changing workplace.

However, business leaders have alienated many educators in the process. It's certainly true that educators have difficulty with the concept of for-profit schools and tough new accountability measures, and many still do not understand the implications for education of the new economic realities. But differences about these ideas do not explain the enmity between the two groups.

The problem is that business leaders often sound as though they know more about how to "run the business of education" than educators do. An axiom in successful businesses today is that the people closest to the problem know the most about how to solve it. If this wisdom is good enough for business, then why isn't it good enough for education? Why did the first two National Governor's Summits on Education include major business leaders, but no educators? (The most recent one had only a token representation of educators.) What kind of message does that send to the education profession? *What would business leaders think if educators sponsored a national summit on the future of business, but did not invite any businesspeople to the event?*

So the first thing business leaders—like politicians—must do is stop giving the impression that they have all the answers. Then they, too, must enter into a dialogue with educators to better understand the major issues in education and to problem solve together.

In addition to continuing to inform educators and parents about the skills most needed in the workplace today, business leaders have several important new leadership opportunities, I believe. They can help to promote better standards and assessments and contribute significantly to the urgent human capital needs in schools in several ways.

Promoting Better Standards and Assessments

I have one simple request to make of CEOs like Lewis Gerstner, chairman of IBM and a leading proponent of new state standards and tests: Take the test! Yes, try taking some of the new state standardized high school level tests, which their lobbying has helped to put into place in most states. And then take *my* simple quiz. Answer the following multiple-choice question:

Based on results from this test, how confident would you be in hiring someone who scored above average?

(a) Completely confident

(b) Very confident

(c) Somewhat confident

(d) Not very confident

(e) None of the above—the test doesn't measure the skills I need

I will be very surprised if the answer is (a) or (b). I would also be surprised if many CEOs are able to pass some states' math exams. A large majority of well-educated adults who have taken the Massachusetts tenth-grade math test were not able to pass it, according to several media reports.

If business leaders answer my quiz honestly, the large majority would say "none of the above." Successful companies do not rely on the kinds of verbal and numerical achievement tests that are now the norm in education. They have learned that such assessments do not measure the skills most needed in today's workplace.

In their book *Teaching the New Basic Skills*, Murnane and Levy report that companies as diverse as Diamond-Star, Honda, and Northwestern Mutual now use interviews and highly sophisticated new simulations to assess applicants' skills on the things that matter most. Diamond-Star did a validity study which showed that "once reading and math scores on paper-and-pencil tests are above a certain threshold, the soft skills—teamwork and communication skills—are the best predictors of (job) performance, and these cannot be detected on multiple choice tests."[1]

Some business schools are also realizing that applicants' scores on traditional graduate school entrance exams tell them nothing about a student's potential to contribute to a business. The *New York Times* recently reported that the University of Michigan Business School is developing a new test that assesses applicants' practical intelligence and problem-solving capability. The test "aims to gauge who is able to learn from mistakes, handle changing situations and cope with less-than-perfect information—the same challenges, its designers say, that working people face every day."[2]

Why should "best practice" assessment in the business world be any different from what's needed in public education? Having been largely responsible for the imposition of new state standards and tests, business leaders must now work with policy makers to convince the public that we need to create much more sophisticated performance-based assessments of students' capabilities, as well as new accountability systems and incentives for educators.

Contributing to the Development of Human Capital in Schools

Perhaps because they have already received too much unsolicited and uninformed advice about how to run their schools, most educators ask businesses for money—and nothing more. But in my experience, what businesses can contribute to the development of human capital in schools may be at least as important as increased financial support.

Lacking opportunities to work in a team setting, most educators have not developed some of the critical people skills needed to lead a change process. Many don't know how to run a good meeting or develop focused strategies for improvement. There is a great deal that businesspeople might teach educators, provided that they are also willing to learn. In my study of school-business partnerships in Massachusetts, I found that both educators and business leaders benefited greatly from the involvement of businesspeople on school improvement teams. Educators learned new skills, while individuals from the business world gained a much deeper understanding of the problems faced by educators.[3]

Another study I completed for the Polaroid Corporation documented how much educators learned from opportunities to work in companies for a semester or a year. High school science teachers reported that after spending a year working at Polaroid, they returned to the classroom with a much deeper appreciation of the corporate world, as well as a new understanding of the skills most needed by students. Many completely rewrote their curriculums, as a result of their experiences, making the learning of science much more connected to the ways in which it might be used in the real world. These teachers also gained a new appreciation for corporate-style teamwork and found it difficult to go back to the isolation of their classrooms.[4]

In addition to these kinds of skill transfers, business leaders can encourage parents and other employees to be more involved in their local schools through more progressive leave policies. Every business should allow parents to take time off for school conferences during the day. They can also encourage all employees to volunteer time in schools to read to children or be a mentor to young adults. Timberland Corporation, for example, provides every employee with one week of paid "community service" leave each year, in addition to regular vacation benefits.

Many businesses offer internships to high school students. These opportunities for "real-world" learning are indispensable to students' understanding of the skills needed in the adult world and, thus, to their motivation to learn. Both for-profit and nonprofit organizations need to work with schools to expand these opportunities and make them available to every student.

Another important contribution to schools that business leaders can make is to ensure that laws limiting students' work hours are strictly enforced. In one Ohio community where I recently consulted, we discovered that many adolescents were working forty-hour weeks, and they often did not get home until quite late on school nights. High school had become just a part-time job for them. These employment practices were widespread, despite the state law, which prohibited students from working more than twenty hours a week.

AFFIRMING THE IMPORTANCE OF CITIZENSHIP COMPETENCIES

One final reason why many educators do not trust business leaders is that they seem only interested in developing workplace skills in order to increase their profits. The problem is twofold.

First, too many educators still do not understand that the skills needed in today's economy are essentially no different from those needed for further learning. They assume that business leaders are only talking about vocational education—learning how to weld so you can build a better car for GM. So business leaders have to continue to help educators and parents understand the core intellectual competencies and people skills most needed in a knowledge economy.

But the other factor that contributes to the mistrust is business leaders' almost complete silence on the topic of education for citizenship. I understand that business has a vested interest in creating a more highly skilled workforce—and quickly. But as citizens we all have an interest in devoting time and attention to preparing students for their civic roles in a democracy.

THE EDUCATIONAL LEADERSHIP WE NEED

Thus far, we've discussed the new kinds of political and business leadership needed to provide incentives and supports for the creation of New Village Schools. But even under the best of circumstances, it may take us a decade or more to develop the policies and public support for education reinvention at a significant scale. So the question remains: Can educational leaders lead a successful "reinvention" process within existing schools and districts? If so, then what are the obstacles and most effective strategies? What are the essential tasks for education leaders today?

In his book *Leadership without Easy Answers*, Ron Heifetz argues that deep, substantive (or what he calls "adaptive") change requires a kind of leadership very different from what is required to make merely incremental (or "technical") improvements. He points out that organizations often lack the knowledge needed to create the more substantive kinds of change. They have to create it. Leaders, alone, do not usually have the new knowledge needed to solve entirely new and much more complex problems. Thus the central task of leaders, Heifetz writes, is to give the problem to the workers through a very different approach to leadership.

Nowhere is this truer than in education. As I've said, one cannot find a school district in America (or in any other country) where all students—or even most students—are learning the skills needed today for work, continuous learning, and citizenship. We have some good individual schools, but we do not have models of public education systems that give all students a high-quality education. We only know how to sort students. The problem is not reform; it is reinvention or redesign.

And so the first request that I have made of political and business leaders is also the most urgent challenge for educational leaders: they need to stop offering simplistic or formulaic solutions to what is, in fact, a brand new and extremely difficult education dilemma. Only then can education leaders go on to consider their most important challenge: how to create a culture that generates new knowledge to solve new problems.

CREATING A "KNOWLEDGE-GENERATING CULTURE"

First-Tier versus Second-Tier Change

In recent school reform efforts, the overwhelming majority of school principals and superintendents have relied on what I call Second-Tier strategies to create change. Second-Tier change efforts attempt to teach people new or improved skills without altering—or even discussing—the organizational culture of the school or district. For example, principals are asked to sit through daylong programs on new leadership styles. And teachers dutifully attend workshops on new approaches to teaching reading and writing. But the skills taught rarely translate into significant changes in schools or improvements in student learning.

When these efforts fail, the conventional thinking is that the principals or teachers didn't have enough time to learn the lesson. So now the trend is to provide more time to educators for this kind of "professional development." But in my experience the reasons why educators do not often improve their skills has less to do with the time allotted than with the culture of the organization and the incentives or disincentives for adult learning and what I call educational research and development.

The problem is that the culture of public schools and district bureaucracies is almost universally based on *compliance*—obeying the rules of authorities and doing only the minimum needed to "get by." Students do only what is needed to get the grade they want, teachers do only what the principal requires them to do, principals do what the central office tells them to do, and even superintendents must do what the state or federal government says. Indeed, these are the rules of survival in almost all bureaucracies around the world.

A compliance-based system does not reward risk-taking or encourage innovation. As a result, it cannot even begin to create the adult learning or make the kinds of changes most needed in education. It cannot generate new knowledge because all of the rewards and incentives tend to reinforce the status quo.

This pattern of behavior is so deeply ingrained in education that teachers, school principals, or superintendents who try to be innovative in any way are quickly branded as outliers by their peers or supervisors. Even among themselves, innovators joke about practicing "creative noncompliance." Many of the best principals I've known who created substantive change in their buildings all had the same motto: "Never ask for permission—only forgiveness."

My colleagues in the Change Leadership Group at the Harvard Graduate School of Education, Bob Kegan and Lisa Lahey, have developed what they call a "technology" that helps individuals and organizations identify their "immunities to change."[5] Their theory is that organizational change can occur only when the immunities to change are identified.

In a recent workshop with principals and central office administrators in one school district, the organizational immunity to change that emerged after four hours of discussion was fear of some higher authority—a fear that had never been acknowledged or discussed before, yet was pervasive throughout the district. This was true, despite the fact that the superintendent in this district had talked about the need for fundamental change, preached "distributive leadership" as a belief, and encouraged his leaders to take initiative for more than a year.

Individual and organizational behaviors do not change unless leaders consciously and systemically set out to create a new "knowledge-generating" culture rooted in *commitment*, rather than compliance. The shared commitment is not merely to obey or not rock the boat. It is to create collaboratively, through sustained dialogue and inquiry, the new knowledge and skills—both individually and organizationally—that will enable all students to learn at high levels. Creating such a culture is the central task of First-Tier change.

Education leaders need to understand the basic differences between a knowledge-generating school culture versus one that is bureaucratic. The language used, the incentives, the relationships, the nature of the work itself, and the outcomes are fundamentally different in each, as the following table summarizes.

First-Tier change means moving from a bureaucratic school culture to a knowledge-generating culture. What drives the change are transformations in the components of culture, outlined in the lefthand column.

THE CULTURAL DRIVERS	A KNOWLEDGE-GENERATING SCHOOL CULTURE	A BUREAUCRATIC SCHOOL CULTURE
Relationships	Highly collaborative and collegial	Isolated and competitive
Responsibility	Shared	Blame others
Motivation	Relationship-driven	Rule-driven
Agreements	Covenants	Contracts
Accountability	Face-to-face, commitment-driven	Anonymous, compliance-based
Learning	Sustained support for individual and organizational learning	Limited and sporadic attention to skill development
Expertise	Collaboratively developed and widely shared	Private and hierarchial
Outcomes	Generation of new knowledge and solutions	Passive or partial replication of old/others' ideas

Responding to Educators' Resistances to Change

How do education leaders undertake successful First-Tier change to create a knowledge-generating culture—driven by commitment rather than compliance? Efforts to answer this question are still comparatively new. However, in my recent consulting work and through conversations with a few courageous education leaders, I have identified what I think are some of the critical elements of success.

The first question that any theory of change should address is: What motivates adults to want to do new and sometimes very difficult things? This question is especially critical in education, as I believe that the temperament, training, and working conditions of most teachers predispose them *not* to want to change. On the other hand, leaders are often individuals who *like* change and so see teachers' reticence to change as sheer stubbornness or indifference. In my experience, most teachers are neither stubborn nor indifferent, but they do resist change for reasons that leaders must understand. Described below are three traits that I find characterize many in our profession; these traits tend to reinforce the existence of compliance-based, bureaucratic school and district cultures.

1. Risk Aversion

Historically, most people have entered the teaching profession because it was a career that promised a high degree of order, security, and stability. In my experience, most experienced educators are risk-averse by temperament, while many who thrive in the business world are risk-seekers. I believe this fundamental difference in temperament is one reason why the two groups generally do not understand or even like one another, and this lack of understanding and communication contributes greatly to the absence of a more thoughtful, balanced dialogue about educational improvement.

The training and working conditions of most teachers have only reinforced this risk aversion. Schools of education foster docility with too many lecture courses and too few opportunities for problem solving, critical thinking, or original thinking, and school district leadership rewards compliance rather than creativity and initiative. The educational fads that have swept through schools for the past thirty years have served to reinforce the belief of many teachers that innovations are the fleeting fancy of leaders who are here today and gone tomorrow—and so are not to be believed.

2. "Craft" Expertise

In traditional cultures, many individuals worked alone as farmers and craftsmen. Historically, education has also been a "craftsman's" trade—attracting people who enjoy working alone and take great pride in developing a degree of expertise and perfecting handcrafted "products." For many teachers, their special unit or course—Native Americans, Shakespeare, AP biology, and so on—represents expertise they have developed over years and is a source of enormous pride. Their greatest sense of job satisfaction is often derived from introducing just a few students to their "craft." Teachers have told me that asking them to give up teaching such a unit is like telling them to cut out a part of what makes them unique as a human being. And many perceive the call to create uniform standards as a demand that everyone teach the same thing in the same way. Their sense of craft pride is offended and their identity threatened.

3. Autonomy and Isolation

Risk aversion and craft pride create a *reticence* to change for many, but it is the autonomy and isolation of educators that limit their *capacity* to change. Craftspeople often have a temperamental predisposition for autonomy, but they are not necessarily isolated in the way that many teachers are. Educators are, first, isolated from the fast-changing world of globalization and business innovation. Most do not understand the fundamental changes that have taken place in the world of work—changes that require that students have very different skills to be successful than those required a quarter-century ago. Lacking daily exposure in their own workplace to these deep-seated economic changes, most educators do not understand the urgency of many business and political leaders.

Educators—who spend most of their workday with children—are also largely isolated from contact with other adults. The physical layout of schools is like an egg crate, with each person working in an isolated cell, and it reinforces autonomy rather than collaboration. With few opportunities to work with or even see other adults during their day in passing, many educators have not developed the skills of teamwork.

Fifty years ago, the opportunity to work alone for most of the day was considered a plus for many adults in our society. Autonomy equaled independence. Not so today. The problems and challenges in the workplaces of the twenty-first century are impossible to solve alone. That's one reason why teamwork is now the dominant mode of work nearly everywhere—except in education. But teachers, working alone, cannot possibly solve the systemic problem of how to get more students to achieve higher standards. Add to this the tendency of leaders to blame educators for what they describe as the "failure" of American education, and I find that most teachers feel both powerless and victimized in their isolation.

Faced with these serious obstacles to change, some leaders—and state legislatures—attempt to apply the most primitive "theory" of human motivation to the problem: they appeal to teachers' fear and greed. They try various forms of intimidation and threaten teachers with the takeover of underperforming schools, or they attempt to bribe them with the promise of bonuses for improved test scores. But most teachers are not moved to do the difficult things required for school change by some combination of threats and bribes. They have tenure and so are not easily threatened, and they are less motivated by the desire for more money than many in other professions.

So if the "carrot-and-stick" theory of human motivation doesn't work, then what does? What motivates teachers? What do leaders need to do to create the will to learn how to improve student achievement?

First, we must acknowledge that most teachers begin with a built-in motivation: they care about students and they want to make a difference. They have what the previously cited Public Agenda Foundation study labeled "a sense of calling." That's one important reason why many chose the profession initially. And so the first challenge in motivating teachers is to help them understand that "making a difference for kids" today requires very different teaching methods and course content than it did when many started their careers a quarter century ago.

But the message can't just be: "Jump higher, do more with less"—which is too often the only message educators hear today. Instead, it must be: "We have a new problem that no one can solve alone. To solve it, we must understand the changing world around us and work collaboratively in order to create new knowledge and skills."

A FRAMEWORK FOR CHANGE AND ADULT LEARNING

There is no question that educators must learn new skills in order to be successful with all students today. But what I am suggesting is that these Second-Tier change efforts must be embedded within, and take place at the same time as, a First-Tier change process that transforms the organizational culture. What, then, does a First-Tier change process look like—change that creates a new knowledge-generating culture and promotes ongoing adult learning?

Just as good teachers create classrooms where students construct new knowledge, leaders must also provide learning opportunities that enable teachers to "construct" a new understanding of the world, their students, and their craft—and thus more deeply understand both the problem and the solution. With this new understanding, leaders can then work with

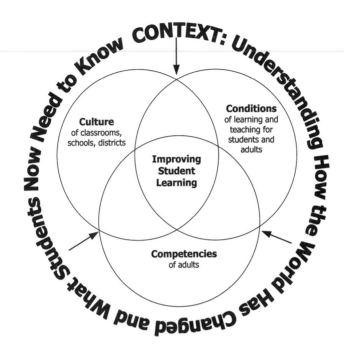

teachers to design the new school structures and conditions that will allow them to be more successful.

What is needed, in a word, is leadership that creates "constructivist" adult learning—dialogue and critical inquiry. What I am describing should not be confused with a simple increased emphasis on professional development—the current fad in schools these days. Leadership for change means creating and sustaining the conditions for continuous adult learning for both teachers and the community—many of whom are as confused and resistant to change as teachers. It means analyzing everything a leader and a school or district does from the point of view of whether or not it is promoting focused, collaborative learning.

In my experience, there are four interrelated tasks in a constructivist change process that results in improved student learning:

1. Understanding *context*: how the world has changed and developing a shared vision and sharp focus on what students need to know that is informed by this understanding

2. Creating a knowledge-generating *culture* based on collaborative inquiry—a culture that encourages new kinds of motivations and relationships, as we saw in the last table

3. Changing the *conditions* of teaching and learning to allow more time for adult collaboration, development of longer-term student-teacher relationships, and more opportunities for individualized learning

4. Developing the *competencies* of teachers and educational leaders to collaborate, identify, and solve problems and initiate and assess more effective teaching strategies

The figure attempts to represent the relationship among these tasks.

Understanding how the world has changed and what students need to know is the overarching framework that develops the necessary focus for the three tasks of creating a knowledge-generating *culture*, changing the *conditions* of teaching and learning, and developing the *competencies* of educators. Improved student achievement is the result of a sustained and coherent approach to these three core tasks. Let me explain each further with some examples.

1. Understanding the *Context* of Education: How the World Has Changed and Developing Vision of What Students Need to Know

My experience is that too many leaders skip over or rush the process of helping teachers and the community really understand the educational "problem." But without a clear understanding of the challenges we face, we have no criteria for determining success or evaluating alternative strategies. Even more significantly, the popular misconception of our educational problem contributes greatly to teachers' sense of victimization and resistance to change, as we have discussed.

Understanding the Need for Change

Why do we need change in schools? When I have asked education leaders— policy makers, superintendents, principals, and school board members—this question, I have often been surprised at how thin and inarticulate their responses are. How can teachers be motivated to change if leaders cannot clearly explain why it is important?

In my work, I have found that making the distinction between "failure" and "obsolescence" is critical for educators' understanding and receptivity to change. Education leaders need to help both teachers and parents understand the kinds of changes we discussed earlier: fundamental changes in the nature of work, in our understanding of what must be taught and how, and in expectations for citizenship.

We also saw that changes in all students' life circumstances and motivations for learning represent perhaps the greatest dilemma for many teachers and are much less well understood. The traditional motivations for learning, the "sticks and carrots" teachers have relied on to get generations of students through school—fear and respect for authority and the belief that sustained hard work equals success and happiness—don't have much meaning for many young people today.

How do education leaders foster this understanding? Not from panels of "experts" lecturing—one of the Second-Tier strategies for change that is widely used and largely ineffectual. In fact, as we've seen, teachers, parents, and community members in diverse communities can best come to this new understanding by "constructing" this knowledge themselves in focused, small group discussions. Individuals have pieces of the knowledge of the change that is all around us. They need time to reflect together to make the pieces whole and to consider the implications for education.

Second, leaders must make the problem a shared responsibility and "blame free." They must make clear that the serious issues we face in schools are not the fault of teachers. Nor are parents and students to blame. In the Harvard Institute for School Leadership, where I have taught for the past five summers, "No shame, no blame, no excuses!" has become our credo.

Finally, leaders need to create time for educators to understand and discuss different kinds of data. Detailed student achievement data that are analyzed according to race and gender is obviously a starting point, as are dropout and ninth-grade failure rates, and so on. But these alone don't often persuade educators that there's a serious problem. The numbers are, after all, nothing new.

Teachers can gather and understand qualitative data, as well. They need to hear the voices of employers talking about the skills needed in the workplace today. They need to hear recent graduates talk about how unprepared they were for work and further learning. And they need to hear current students talk about the problem of lack of teacher respect for students and how cold and uncaring most schools seem. Although more time-consuming to collect, this kind of data—presented through panel discussions, videos of focus groups, and so on—often creates the sense of urgency many teachers need in order to begin to take risks and try new things in their classrooms.

Developing a Shared Vision of What Students Need to Know

For many leaders, a shared vision begins and ends with a school or district mission statement stuck to a bulletin board somewhere. They've become de rigueur in most businesses, so educators feel they must have them too.

However, as a tool in the change process, such statements are virtually useless.

In chapter 2, I argued that we need clarity about what are the few most important things students should know and be able to do—a short list of expectations for all students that grows out of a new awareness of how the world has changed and the essential skills needed for work, continuous learning, and citizenship today.

Then we need a deeper, shared understanding of the good teaching practices that can achieve those goals and the performance-based assessments that best measure student progress—topics we considered in chapters 3 and 4. In both chapters, we saw examples of education leaders who created community discussions for consensus on key learning priorities: what few things are most important for all students to know and be able to do.

With a much sharper vision of what is most important to learn, educators are in a stronger position to explore "best practices" in teaching. But here again, the task of a leader is not to tell teachers what these are, but to create the opportunities for educators to discover them for themselves. A short lecture on group work or a motivational speaker on how all students can learn do not persuade veterans who have spent years honing their craft expertise to try something new.

Effective leaders give teams of experienced teachers—the leaders in the school buildings—time to visit successful schools and to discuss what they've learned with colleagues. Teachers need to see models of much more successful classrooms in order to believe that all students can succeed. Over time and with a well-planned and well-funded program of peer supervision, this general understanding of best practice evolves into a more specific set of skills that the teachers in every building master and then pass on to others as the new craft expertise, as we will soon see in the example of PS 198.

2. Creating a Knowledge-Generating *Culture*

I have argued earlier in this chapter that creating a knowledge-generating school and district culture is a precondition for successful school reinvention. Once leaders learn to resist the temptation of offering easy answers and, instead, learn to frame the key challenges and questions for groups to work on, then the next task is to work on relationships. Relationships based on compliance—with little or no respect—are often the first problem to tackle in a school change process, and collaborative relationships based on trust and respect are the foundation of a knowledge-generating culture.

The problem of lack of respect in most schools—especially middle and high schools—is profound, as we have seen. The importance of respect in the classroom is probably obvious to most educators—at least in theory. Most students will not work hard for teachers whom they feel do not respect them. And they will not try new things or take risks in classrooms where sarcastic comments are tolerated or—worse—modeled by teachers.

Adult learning and dialogue are similarly inhibited by lack of respect. Younger teachers are often cowed into silence by the snide comments of their older peers in faculty meetings and lunchrooms. Often, it is just one or two cynical teachers who psychologically dominate an entire building and so cut off all meaningful conversation about school improvement.

One of the challenges for leaders is to distinguish between the skeptics and the cynics. They may often sound alike, but in fact they have very different motives. The skeptics are usually experienced and committed educators whose concerns must be understood and addressed, while the cynics are the teachers who have given up and should be removed from the building as quickly as possible.

A strong educational leader makes clear that the creation of a respectful environment for both students and adults is nonnegotiable and is everyone's responsibility. Incivility is not tolerated from anyone. Naming the problem by conducting student focus groups and then creating small group conversations about behaviors of concern and behaviors to be encouraged—both adult and student—is often an important starting point. New peer and school norms, or core values, result from such discussions.

Once a safer, more respectful environment has been established in a school, then leaders can create meaningful tasks or topics, teams, and regular weekly times for discussions. Just as students learn social skills, or EQ, through group work, so, too, do teachers learn how to work more collaboratively through regular problem-solving discussions in small groups. Gradually, the sense of isolation and preference for autonomy give way to pride in the accomplishments of a team—in making more of a difference for students. Over time, teacher groups progress from discussions of curriculum and student work to visiting one another's classes and, finally, to offering critiques of teaching. Creating such a collaborative culture takes years, but ultimately, this kind of peer supervision—not evaluations by leaders—is the key to improving instruction and is at the heart of successful school improvement efforts that I have observed.

Leaders help to establish such a culture by modeling respectful behavior, seeking critical feedback on their performance from teachers (teacher reviews of administrators and student reviews of teachers should be the norm in every school and district), and providing the resources needed—time to work together and released time for master teachers to coach colleagues.

I saw firsthand the importance of changing relationships as a part of creating a knowledge-generating culture in the school improvement process when I was once asked to work in a school where the administration and teachers were at war with one another (which is not at all uncommon) and student learning was substandard. After spending a few days in the school, listening and observing, I concluded that the first step to improving learning was to create more collaborative adult relationships. We began the school improvement process with small-group conversations about adult relationships in the building.

Teachers said that they felt the principal did not respect them. I reported this to the principal and helped her to see how some of her messages and behaviors were conveying this impression. She agreed to work at changing both. But first we had to clear the air. The principal and a half dozen of the most senior teachers agreed to participate in a half-day, off-site retreat with me as a facilitator. We went around the circle and gave each person time to talk about the hurt and misunderstandings that had characterized their relationships. It was a difficult session, and this principal and the teachers showed tremendous courage in their willingness to be more open with one another. Everyone left that day with a willingness to suspend judgment and a desire start over.

Soon after, with my encouragement, the principal established a school improvement committee that had representatives from all grade level teams in the school. Together, as a team, they began to problem solve in new ways and to talk about how to improve teaching and learning. By her actions, the principal demonstrated that she valued teachers' ideas and needed their help. She began to rebuild trust and to develop a culture of collaborative inquiry.

But it wasn't just the administrator-teacher relationships that were problematic in this school. It was also teachers' relationships with their peers. In these same small-group discussions, teachers acknowledged what they called the issue of "parking lot conversations." If a teacher had a concern about what another teacher had said or done with a student, he or she would talk about it to a third teacher—usually in the parking lot. Teachers were afraid to talk face-to-face about issues and differences. The result, of course, was that individuals did not trust one another and so could not collaborate.

As a group, the teachers decided to create what they called new "peer norms." They agreed to end the parking lot conversations and talk *to* one another, rather than *about* one another. After a few months, they checked in during a faculty meeting and concluded that they were not always doing what they had said they would do. Change was hard. Teachers had to learn new skills—how to give constructive but critical feedback. But they knew that it was critical to the school and to their own morale, and so they recommitted to their peer norms.

Two years later—because of the remarkable courage of this principal and group of teachers—the school was a completely different place. Teachers, working together, had developed new and more rigorous graduation requirements for students. The level of teaching in nearly every classroom had improved dramatically as a result of a new peer mentoring program and continuing collaborative conversation about teaching and learning. State test scores had improved significantly. And both student and teacher morale in the building was transformed.

Changing the relationships enabled this group to change the conversation. The topic was no longer what they were doing to each other, but rather how could they work more effectively together for the benefit of all students.

3. Changing the *Conditions* of Teaching and Learning and Developing the *Competencies* of Educators

Understanding how the world has changed, developing from that understanding a shared vision of what students need to know, and creating a *culture* of respectful relationships and collaborative inquiry are all necessary supports for adult learning. This learning develops educators' motivation for thoughtful, responsible risk-taking—educational research and development—and supports the development of craft expertise focused on real competencies for all students. But leaders also need to create strategies for changing the *conditions* of teaching and learning and developing the *competencies* of both teachers and school and district leaders. I'll explain more about changing conditions and developing capacities by way of a case study. It is also a story that shows how all of these elements must work together.

The Story of PS 198

PS 198 is an elementary school in New York City's District 2. When Anthony Alvarado became superintendent there in 1987, District 2, an economically and racially diverse district, was ranked thirteenth in reading test scores in the region. Seven years later, it ranked second, behind a predominantly white, middle-class district. The story of District 2's success is an extraordinary one and has been chronicled by several researchers, notably Richard Elmore at Harvard and Lauren Resnick at the University of Pittsburgh. But the story of PS 198 itself has not been told. It provides a way of understanding the strategies I've listed, which Alvarado and his deputy superintendent, Elaine Fink, used to turn around a school.[6]

PS 198 is a school that serves a large majority of families who live in poverty. More than 90 percent of its students are eligible for free or reduced-fee lunch (a nationally used indicator of poverty in schools). It consistently ranked dead last on reading scores in the district. Alvarado hired a new principal, Gloria Buckerey, in 1996. Buckerey worked hard to weed out incompetent teachers, brought in a couple of staff developers, and hired new young teachers, but few of them lasted more than a year. The job seemed overwhelming.

After three years, nothing had changed. (Leadership, by itself, is not enough!) Only about 25 percent of the fourth-graders were reading at or above grade level on the comparatively easy standardized tests then in use. The problem of poor student achievement and high staff turnover became so severe that the state of New York put PS 198 on its list of Schools Under Review in 1998. Essentially, this meant that if things didn't change quickly, the state would close the school. Alvarado and Fink decided new strategies were needed to turn the situation around, and Fink began visiting the school monthly. Over a period of about six months, she developed an action plan for change.

What Students Need to Know: A Laserlike Focus on Literacy

For the first five years in District 2, the sole focus of school improvement efforts—all staff development, all conversations with principals—was how to improve teaching and learning for literacy. Alvarado reasoned that if students could not read, comprehend, and write well then they certainly were not going to be able to decode math or science texts. And so improving student literacy was Fink's focus in PS 198. She knew that trying to attend to science, social studies, and math skills at the same time would not provide the focus—and the opportunity for success—that teachers needed.

One of the great mistakes of the high-stakes testing movement in my judgment is the attempt to test an ever-increasing number of subject areas as if they all mattered equally. High-level math skills are—foolishly, I think—a requirement for college, but how often are they used by adults in everyday life? By contrast, a high level of literacy—the ability to comprehend complex material, synthesize information, and present it clearly, both orally and in writing—is an indispensable skill in most workplaces today. Literacy and the ability to evaluate data and statistics (rather than do algebra) are also essential for citizenship. If we really want to raise the levels of student achievement quickly, then I believe we need the equivalent of a Marshall Plan to improve literacy. All other high-stakes testing should be suspended for five years.

Changing the Conditions of Teaching and Learning

Too few would-be school reformers pay sufficient attention to the conditions of teaching and learning, in my experience. They think that professional development is the silver bullet that will improve learning all by itself. But the best professional development program in the world will not enable me to teach students to write well if I face 150 anonymous faces a day—as most high school English teachers do.

We need to pay as much attention to improving the conditions of teaching and learning as we do to professional development. If we do not, then educators' motivation to improve will be very limited. They *know* they cannot do what they are being asked to unless the conditions under which they have to work are improved, so why should they bother to learn a new skill? This is especially true at the middle and high school level, but even in elementary schools, the conditions of teaching and learning can often be improved significantly.

The first thing that Fink did was to ask Buckerey, the principal, to work with all the teachers at PS 198 to change the school schedule. She did not try to impose a new one on them, she simply posed the problem for them to solve: How are we going to find more time in the day for literacy instruction and for adult learning? Together, the group created a new schedule that allowed for three-hour literacy blocks in the school day, as well as for a significant increase in time for teacher meetings to talk about their work. The group also decided that the "specialist" teachers—those who taught art, science, music, and so on—would learn how to teach literacy and be an additional resource in the classroom. Finally, Fink assigned two additional reading specialists to the school.

The immediate result of these changes was that every student reading group would now work with a teacher once every day. Previously, students rarely worked with a teacher in this way more than once a week.

Developing the Competencies of Teachers and Principals

When Fink began analyzing the school's reading test data, she quickly realized that three-quarters of the fourth-graders had had beginning teachers for their first three years of school. These inexperienced teachers didn't know how to teach literacy. And since the turnover rate was so high, there were no teachers in the building with literacy instruction skills who could help their less experienced colleagues.

Fink approached the union and suggested that they create a new distinguished teacher position—with extra duties and a higher salary. Two distinguished teachers—the best literacy educators in the district—came to the school and worked alongside regular classroom teachers, modeling how to teach literacy and coaching their peers. These distinguished teachers also worked with all of the staff during the time available for whole school professional development.

While literacy is a nonnegotiable focus in District 2, Alvarado and Fink do not believe that all schools and all students need the exact same curriculum. As Fink said in a recent conversation, "You don't stand in front of your principals and say 'all schools should. . . .' Each school, like each child, has its own unique learning challenges. This is about kids learning; it's not about philosophy. All kids need rigor, but they learn in different ways, need different things."

Fink worked with Buckerey, the distinguished teachers, and the faculty to adapt the "balanced" literacy program that had been developed in the district to the particular needs of the students in PS 198. All teachers now spent a half-hour a day on word study (phonics), in addition to all of the other elements of the literacy program. Gradually, they all learned how to integrate this work into the regular curriculum.

Alvarado asked Fink what else they might need to turn the situation around and, together, they created a summer program for all of the students in PS 198. In the second year, they created a new summer program for all incoming kindergartners, so that they could start school in the fall better prepared. These programs were so successful that they were subsequently adopted throughout the district in those schools serving the most at-risk students.

But the question remained: How could Buckerey and the teachers know if they were making progress? Once again, Fink and the PS 198 team developed an innovation. They began using the same "graded" reading texts with all students, and they created a chart for each student that showed exactly what reading level they had attained. Fink visited every classroom in the school and discussed each student's chart with Buckerey *monthly*. They also reviewed every teacher's individual learning plan and made changes, as needed, according to the students' reading chart progress. These practices, pioneered in PS 198, are now widespread in the district.

Fink tells her principals, "I have failed you if I can't teach you how to teach your teachers." She worked closely with Buckerey to develop her abilities to coach her teachers and run effective staff meetings. She provided time for Buckerey to be in study groups with other principals, to do school visitations, and to work with another principal in the district who was assigned to be her "buddy."

Supports for Teachers

The change effort I describe was intensive—and therefore expensive—and one of Alvarado's tasks was to ensure districtwide support for the effort. He helped other principals to understand that the PS 198's struggle was all of their problem—and no one's fault. Principals of other schools knew that a disproportionate share of the financial resources was going to PS 198, and they supported that decision, as did the board. They also helped their colleagues develop new leadership and supervision skills.

The culture of District 2 bears a close resemblance to the culture of collaborative problem solving and teacher teamwork that has been the primary strategy used in Japan to improve public education. *The Teaching Gap* by James Stigler and James Hiebert, which I mentioned earlier, describes what the Japanese call "the lesson study process," where groups of teachers work together to identify a common learning problem of students and then create a model lesson to solve the problem. Lessons are refined collaboratively and then, when proven successful, are widely disseminated.

I believe that what Alvarado and Fink accomplished as educational leaders was more than just the sum of the Second-Tier change strategies they employed to improve teaching skills. Their work, in my view, is one of the few successful examples of districtwide change that combined all of the elements of the process I have described: Over a period of years, they created a knowledge-generating *culture* where there is now a clear and widely shared *commitment* to providing a quality education for all students, where teachers have *a shared vision* of what is most important to learn (literacy was first, but now they are working on math as well), and where there are powerful collaborative *relationships* based on trust and respect. This work laid the foundation and created the focus for changing the *conditions* of teaching and learning and developing the *competencies* of educators at every level.

Teachers in District 2 sometimes complain about how hard the work is, but they also say they have never been in a place where there was more collaboration, collegiality, and opportunities for professional growth. Teachers have learned how to help *all* students achieve. They are more successful than they ever thought possible.

Together, district leaders, principals, and teachers have learned new skills and created new knowledge—through a process of educational research and development—about how best to ensure that all students learn at high levels. Alvarado and Fink have recently taken up new challenges in San Diego, but they have left behind a culture in District 2 that actively encourages continuous adult learning, dialogue, and research and development around what is called "the work."

What were the results of all these efforts? Two years after PS 198 was put under review by the state, it was taken off the list. By the end of year three of this process, 55 percent of the students were scoring in the top half of a newer and much more difficult literacy test. Their scores were now in the middle range of a district whose test scores are the second highest in the region and whose literacy scores continue to improve every year.

In 2000, Buckerey was honored by the state as the principal who had made the most progress of any leading a School Under Review. And two of Buckerey's teachers had, themselves, become distinguished teachers in District 2.

COMMUNITY ENGAGEMENT: FROM "PR" TO PARTNERSHIP

There is another vital support that educators need, which the story of PS 198 does not highlight—and that is the active involvement of the community in public schools. Throughout this book, I have argued that a different kind of engagement on the part of everyone is needed to transform our schools. While our focus has been how best to motivate students and teachers to achieve at higher levels, parents and the community must also be a part of the solution. We saw how Central Park East Secondary School promoted greater parental involvement through very different approaches to student advising and parent conferences, but how can educational leaders encourage greater community engagement? How might education leaders involve parents and community members in a process that helps them understand the need for new kinds of schools like Central Park East?

"Buy-In" versus Ownership

In collaboration with my colleagues Linda Greyser and Cliff Baden in Programs in Professional Education at the Harvard Graduate School of Education, I developed the Harvard Seminar on Public Engagement. We work with teams from school districts and states over several days to better understand how the public thinks about education issues and how best to involve them in school improvement. At the end of the seminar, I ask individuals to reflect on some of the most important things they've learned and then invite anyone who wishes to share their thoughts. The most frequent comment comes from superintendents who say, "I came here to learn how to tell the public what a good job we're doing. What I learned is the importance of listening to the public and creating dialogue."

An overriding preoccupation of education leaders today is how to get what they routinely call "buy-in" from teachers, parents, and community members. They know they need political and financial support for their school improvement plan or district change strategy in order to succeed, and so many are looking for a better public relations plan—one that will guarantee buy-in from all the "stakeholders."

By contrast, a First-Tier change strategy strives to create community understanding of the education challenges we face. Adult learning is not just for the educators. Most people have not had an opportunity to reflect on the changes that have taken place in our world and what these mean for children and educators. Before community members can be asked to provide increased financial support for education—which is urgently needed—they need opportunities to learn more about the real issues we face in schools today. A greater understanding of the problems can be developed through programs similar to what the superintendent of the Windsor Public Schools did (described in chapter 2). He framed the key challenges and questions, provided opportunities for thoughtful dialogue, and then invited the public to help create the solutions through the development of new education goals and priorities. This sustained engagement process creates real "ownership" of both the problems and the solutions.

For this process to be successful, education leaders have to give up two common misconceptions: first, the belief that they are the experts with all the answers; and second, the idea that all they need from the public to be successful is more political and financial support—more time and money.

LEARNING COMMUNITIES AS THE NEW VILLAGE COMMONS

It has been the thesis of this book that we face essentially two new problems in American public education: we must educate *all* students for the *new* workplace competencies, as well as for continuous learning and citizenship, and we must find new ways to motivate *all* students to want to achieve these competencies and to succeed in school. Education today, more than ever before, must actively engage all students.

The problem of student motivation is more complex today because of changes in children's life circumstances, but, in fact, educators have never been able to motivate all students to want to achieve without help from parents and community members. We have always needed to work in partnership—something too many education leaders forget in their rush to secure increased political and financial support. Certainly we need more time and money to transform American public education, but these alone are not enough to accomplish the task.

The play *Our Town* by Thornton Wilder depicts life in a typical New England town in an earlier and simpler era. Education of the young there was a seamless partnership between teachers, parents, extended family, neighbors, and community members. Everyone considered himself or herself a teacher of the young.

Is such shared responsibility a middle-class white fantasy? Not according to Dr. James Comer, a prominent African-American psychiatrist at Yale University. He describes his own childhood, growing up in an American urban ghetto in the 1940s, where adults shared responsibility for the care and mentoring of all young people. To Dr. Comer, having this safety net made the critical difference. Ernesto Cortes, a MacArthur Foundation Fellowship winner and organizer for the Industrial Areas Foundation, describes very similar experiences growing up in San Antonio, Texas. For the past twenty years, both Comer and Cortes have, each in their own ways, worked to develop new approaches to school improvement. Their highly effective models of change are based on the premise that teachers, parents, and community members must form new partnerships to ensure that all children learn both the intellectual and social skills they need.[7]

The ultimate goal of a successful public engagement effort, then, is to re-create voluntary communities, centered on the activities of student *and* adult learning, in order to rebuild what many now call "social capital." Cortes describes social capital as a "measure of how much collaborative time and energy people have for each other, how much time parents have for their children, how much attention neighbors will give to each other's families, what kind of relationships people in congregations have with each other, . . . and the quality of many other potential webs of relationships in a community."[8]

But today most people live far from the communities where they were raised. And so we must create a different kind of community in order to replenish our depleted supply of social capital—communities that are more intentional and not necessarily defined by geography. We need a New Village Commons that surrounds and supports New Village Schools.

Historically, most communities were created by accident. They were usually the result of some physical proximity or immediate shared need. Sometimes they furthered the goals of the growth and development of their members, sometimes they didn't—as any long-time resident of a small town will tell you.

By contrast, an "intentional community" is created for a purpose. In fact, the term "intentional community" was first widely used to describe efforts of the nineteenth-century utopians to create communities whose goal was the intellectual and spiritual growth of all its members. The best way to understand Central Park East Secondary School and many of the kindred schools described in the last chapter is to see them as "intentional learning communities" *for both students and adults.*

Such learning communities generate very different kinds of commitments and behaviors from all shareholders. The spirit of the community is one of shared responsibility and collaborative inquiry. Everyone's voice is valued. Each person or group's contribution is essential. And learning and sharing are ongoing and not just confined to students or to the classroom.

Developing such a learning community requires a leader with qualities of heart and mind very different from the traditional role models. To get significantly better schools for all students, good management is not enough, and charisma can get in the way. Today's successful educational leaders understand that they cannot mandate change. They motivate groups to learn and problem solve together by framing the big challenges and asking tough questions, while refusing to offer easy answers. They are self-aware and reflective, seek constructive criticism, and freely admit mistakes. They are leaders who, above all, model good teaching and learning every day.

However, there are far too few of them. Can more of our educational leaders overcome what I call "answeritis" and learn to say, "I don't know"? Can they learn to trust groups of teachers, parents, and community members to find the best solutions to the pressing challenges of "education reinvention"? Are they willing to take risks, themselves, and become learners and co-collaborators? The future of American public education may well depend on growing numbers of leaders who respond to these new challenges with a confident "yes!" and who have the courage to act on their convictions.

But they will need allies. They cannot do this work alone. The future of American education also depends on having more political, business, and community leaders—as well as citizens and parents—who are willing to enter into a sustained dialogue and share the work with educators, where each learns from the other and all contribute to meeting the needs of the next generation.

In the process of coming together to support New Village Schools, we may also create new connections and meaning for ourselves, as adults. For it isn't just students and teachers who need learning communities. As the work of Amitai Etzioni, founder of the Communitarian Network suggests, many of us long for new forms of community in our lives.[9] The yearning for community may be one of the few things on which conservatives and liberals, older and younger generations, businesspeople and educators, men and women can agree. The phenomenal growth of adult study circles and reading groups in recent years testifies to the power of learning communities.

We need adult learning communities as a counterpoint to our highly individualistic and often materialistic daily routines. The life-giving energy that flows from shared learning and creation is the alternative to an isolated "life style" of passive consumption, as psychoanalyst Erich Fromm wrote nearly fifty years ago.[10] In working together to nurture New Village Schools, we may come to rediscover common ground: a New Village Commons whose transcendent purpose is an intertwining of the shared stewardship of the young with our own adult development.

Curious, alive, always learning, growing. The New Village School and the New Village Commons, each inspiring the other. Together, they voice a stronger and more vibrant answer to the question of what it means to be an educated adult in the twenty-first century.

The 1983 National Commission on Excellence in Education report set off the current firestorm of school reform by claiming that our nation was "at risk."[11] The report argued that we were committing "unilateral educational disarmament" through the persistence of low standards in our schools. Because of our poor education system, we were falling dangerously behind other nations economically—and so were at risk strategically as well, the authors suggested. But our nation is not at risk today in the ways that were claimed. The Cold War is over, and our economy is the strongest in the world. Thus, the time to reassess our risk and redefine our education goals is long overdue.

Indeed, we are still a nation at risk, but it is our children and their future that are more at risk than our economy or national security. Many students who go to American public schools today are very much at risk, especially poor and minority children. They are at risk of graduating without the skills needed today for work, lifelong learning, citizenship, and personal growth and health. They are at risk of leaving high school without once experiencing the joy of learning or connecting with a caring adult. They are at risk because their lives are all too often lacking in purpose or direction, meaning, and hope. And with so many of our children at risk in these ways, our future as a nation is also at risk. These children are *our* future. We have no other.

We know how to create truly good schools—New Village Schools that inspire both hearts and minds. We know what they look like, how they work, how they can be held accountable—and how much better the results are for all the students who attend these schools. We also know that, by becoming a focus for community, they enrich the lives of many adults as well.

Yes, we know the way, but reinvention feels risky and is much harder to initiate than mere reform. It's so much simpler just to pass a law and make up another test. So now the real question is: Can we summon and sustain the will?

Our children are counting on us.

NOTES

INTRODUCTION: WHAT'S REALLY WRONG WITH OUR SCHOOLS?

1. See Richard Rothstein, *The Way We Were? The Myths and Realities of American Student Achievement* (New York: The Century Foundation Press, 1998), chapter 4.

2. As reported in an Associated Press wire article, September 15, 2000.

3. See Drew Lindsay, "Call to Arms," *Teacher Magazine*, April 2000, p. 19.

4. Gary Orfield and Johanna Wald, "Testing, Testing," *Nation*, June 5, 2000.

5. Walt Haney, "The Myth of the Texas Miracle in Education," *Education Policy Analysis Archives* v. 8, no. 41, August 19, 2000, http://epaa.asu.edu/epaa/v8n41/.

6. As reported in the October 24, 2000, *New York Times*.

7. The Education Trust, *High Schools in America* (Washington, DC: Education Trust, 2000).

8. Public Agenda Foundation, "Issue Guide," Public Agenda Online, May 26, 2000, http://www.publicagenda.org/issues/frontdoor.cfm?issue_type=family.

9. Public Agenda Foundation, *First Things First: What Americans Expect from the Public Schools* (New York: Public Agenda, 1994).

10. Public Agenda Foundation, "Reality Check 2000," *Education Week*, February 16, 2000.

11. *New York Times*, September 3, 2000.

CHAPTER 1: HOW HAS THE WORLD CHANGED FOR CHILDREN?

1. This quote and the subsequent data are from Richard Murnane and Frank Levy, *Teaching the New Basic Skills* (New York: The Free Press, 1996), chapter 2.

2. As quoted in "Making Sense of the Stubborn Education Gap," *New York Times*, July 23, 2000.

3. Ibid.

4. Howard Gardner, *The Unschooled Mind: How Children Think and How Schools Should Teach* (New York: Basic Books, 1991), chapters 8 and 9.

5. The data and quotes in this section are from Robert Putnam, *Bowling Alone:*

The Collapse and Revival of American Community (New York: Simon & Schuster, 2000), chapters 2 and 3.

6. Theodore R. Sizer and Nancy F. Sizer, *The Students Are Watching* (Boston: Beacon Press, 2000).

7. This and the data in the following paragraph are from Public Agenda Foundation, *Playing Their Parts: Parents and Teachers Talk about Parental Involvement in Schools* (New York: Public Agenda, 1999).

8. This quote and the following data are from Mihaly Csikszentmihalyi and Reed Larson, *Being Adolescent: Conflict and Growth in the Teenage Years* (New York: Basic Books, 1984), chapter 4.

CHAPTER 2: WHAT DO TODAY'S STUDENTS NEED TO KNOW?

1. Massachusetts State Department of Education, *Five Year Plan* (Malden, MA, 1994).

2. Public Agenda Foundation, "Reality Check 2000," *Education Week*, February 16, 2000.

3. Hugh B. Price, "The Aim of Urban School Reform: Successful Schools, Not 'Systemic' Reform," unpublished paper, October 12, 1999.

4. Bill & Melinda Gates Foundation, "District Grant Application Guidelines," http://www.gatesfoundation.org/learning/education/schoolgrantdefault.htm.

5. See E. D. Hirsch, *Cultural Literacy: What Every American Needs to Know* (Boston: Houghton Mifflin, 1987).

6. Public Agenda Foundation, *Assignment Incomplete: The Unfinished Business of Education Reform* (New York: Public Agenda, 1995).

7. Public Agenda Foundation, *First Things First: What Americans Expect from the Public Schools* (New York: Public Agenda, 1994).

8. See Robert Coles, *Privileged Ones: The Well-Off and the Rich in America* (Boston: Little, Brown, 1977).

9. See Daniel Yankelovich, *Coming to Public Judgment: Making Democracy Work in a Complex World* (Syracuse, NY: Syracuse University Press, 1991).

10. See Daniel Yankelovich, *The Magic of Dialogue* (New York: Simon & Schuster, 1999).

CHAPTER 3: HOW DO WE HOLD STUDENTS AND SCHOOLS ACCOUNTABLE?

1. My summary of the Central Park East Secondary School story is taken from Deborah Meier's wonderful book, *The Power of Their Ideas* (Boston: Beacon Press, 1996).

2. Ibid., p. 170.

3. Quoted from a study by Linda Darling-Hammond and Jacqueline Ancess,

Graduation by Portfolio at Central Park East Secondary School (New York: NCREST, 1994).

4. Quoted from the Chugach School District Report Card (Anchorage, AK: Chugach School District, June 2000).

5. See David Bensman, *Learning to Think Well: Central Park East Secondary School Graduates Reflect on Their High School and College Experiences* (New York: NCREST, 1995).

6. Jacqueline Ancess, *Outside/Inside, Inside/Outside: Developing and Implementing the School Quality Review* (New York: NCREST, 1996).

7. The National Commission on Governing America's Schools, *Governing America's Schools: Changing the Rules* (Denver, CO: Education Commission of the States, 1999).

CHAPTER 4: WHAT DO "GOOD SCHOOLS" LOOK LIKE?

1. My description of Central Park East Secondary School and the ideas that have influenced its development are based on a number of sources: Deborah Meier, *The Power of Their Ideas* (Boston: Beacon Press, 1996); numerous conversations with Meier; a visit to the school; a book by George Wood, *Schools That Work* (New York: Dutton, 1992); and an excellent documentary video directed by Frederic Weisman, *High School II.*

2. Public Agenda Foundation, *Getting By: What American Teenagers Really Think about Their Schools* (New York: Public Agenda, 1997).

3. For individuals interested in learning more about how school schedules can be organized to reduce the student load, please see the Appendix to *Horace's School* (Boston: Houghton Mifflin, 1994), by Theodore R. Sizer, as well as George Wood's excellent guide to high school "reinvention," *A Time to Learn* (New York: Penguin, 1998).

4. *Encarta® World English Dictionary* (Bellevue, WA: Microsoft Corporation, 1999).

5. John I. Goodlad, *A Place Called School: Prospects for the Future* (New York: McGraw-Hill, 1984), p. 229.

6. For more information, see the City Year website: http://www.cityyear.org/.

7. The data, tables, and quotes in this section are from Public Agenda Foundation, *A Sense of Calling* (New York: Public Agenda, 2000).

8. David W. Grissmer, Ann Flanagan, Jennifer Kawata, and Stephanie Willimson, *Improving Student Achievement: What NAEP State Test Scores Tell Us* (Santa Monica: Rand Corporation, 2000), http://www.rand.org/publications/MR/MR924/.

9. *Education Week*, August 2, 2000.

10. As reported in the March 19, 1999, issue of *Education Week*.

11. Meier, *The Power of Their Ideas*, p. 108.

12. Ibid., p. 109.

13. There are more than ten years of research showing the benefits to students of smaller schools. For a summary of this research, see Mary Anne Raywid, "Small Schools, A Reform That Works," *Educational Leadership*, December 1997. See also a recent comprehensive study conducted by Pat Wasley and others, *Small Schools, Great Strides* (New York: Bank Street College of Education, 2000).

14. At the Grantmakers in Education panel presentation (Boston, MA, November 8, 2000).

15. Meier, *The Power of Their Ideas*, p. 110.

16. Ibid., p. 110.

17. See the small schools research cited in above.

18. The Institute for Education and Social Policy, *The Effects of Size of Student Body on School Costs and Performance in New York City High Schools* (New York: New York University, 1998).

19. The story of Julia Richman is based on visits to the school, conversations with Ann Cook, as well as her chapter in *Creating New Schools*, edited by Evans Clinchy (New York: Teachers College Press, 2000). Evaluation data for the experiment are reported by Linda Darling Hammond and her colleagues in another chapter of the same book.

20. See the website, http://www.gatesfoundation.org/learning/education/districtcriteria.htm.

21. As reported in the December 28, 2000, issue of the *New York Times*.

22. United States Department of Education, *The State of Charter Schools 2000—Fourth-Year Report, January 2000* (Washington, DC: Publisher, 2000).

CHAPTER 5: WHAT MUST LEADERS DO?

1. Richard Murnane and Frank Levy, *Teaching the New Basic Skills* (New York: The Free Press, 1996), p. 37.

2. David Leonhardt, "Management: On Testing for Common Sense; A Business School Thinks It Makes Sense. Yes? No?" *New York Times*, May 24, 2000.

3. See my report, *Carnegie School-Business Partnerships: A Report on the First Year* (Boston: Massachusetts State Department of Education, 1990).

4. See my study, *Straddling Two Cultures: Polaroid's Project Bridge and School Reform* (Cambridge, MA: Polaroid Corporation, 1991).

5. See Robert Kegan and Lisa Laskow Lahey, *How the Way We Talk Can Change the Way We Work: Seven Languages for Transformation* (San Francisco: Jossey-Bass, 2000).

6. This account is based on a presentation by Anthony Alvarado and Elaine Fink at the Grantmakers in Education conference (Boston, MA, November 7, 2000) and subsequent conversations with both Alvarado and Fink. Alvarado served as superintendent in New York City's Community District 2 from 1987 until 1998 and was suc-

ceeded by his colleague Fink. They are now both working in the San Diego Public Schools. District 2 is widely considered one of the very few districts in the country that has significantly raised the achievement levels of nearly every student. I am indebted to Elaine and Tony for opportunities to learn from them through many thought-provoking conversations as well as several visits to District 2.

7. For a description of Dr. Comer's approach to school improvement, see his recent book, *Waiting for a Miracle* (New York: Dutton, 1997); see also Ernesto Cortes, Jr., "Making the Public the Leaders in Education Reform," *Education Week*, November 22, 1995, http://www.edweek.org/ew/vol-15/12cortes.h15.

8. Ernesto Cortes, Jr., in Henry G. Cisneros, ed., *Interwoven Destinies: Cities and the Nation* (New York: W.W. Norton & Company, 1993), pp. 295–319.

9. See Amitai Etzioni, *The Spirit of Community* (New York: Simon & Schuster, 1993).

10. Erich Fromm's many books offer profound insights into the dangers of a society or a life centered around consumption. *The Sane Society* (New York: Holt, Rinehart, & Winston, 1955) and *To Have or to Be* (New York: Harper & Row, 1976) are two of his books that deal most directly with these topics.

11. National Commission on Excellence in Education, *A Nation at Risk: The Imperative for Educational Reform* (Washington, DC: U.S. GPO, 1983.)

BIBLIOGRAPHY

Jacqueline Ancess, *Outside/Inside, Inside/Outside: Developing and Implementing the School Quality Review* (New York: NCREST, 1996).

John Chubb and Terry Moe, *Politics, Markets, and America's Schools* (Washington, DC: Brookings Institution, 1990).

Evans Clinchy, ed., *Creating New Schools: How Small Schools Are Changing American Education* (New York: Teachers College Press, 2000).

James Comer, *Waiting for a Miracle* (New York: Dutton, 1997).

Mihaly Csikszentmihalyi and Reed Larson, *Being Adolescent: Conflict and Growth in the Teenage Years* (New York: Basic Books, 1984).

Linda Darling-Hammond and Jacqueline Ancess, *Graduation by Portfolio at Central Park East Secondary School* (New York: NCREST, 1994).

Edward B. Fiske and Helen F. Ladd, *When Schools Compete: A Cautionary Tale* (Washington, DC: Brookings Institution, 2000).

Howard Gardner, *Frames of Mind* (New York: Basic Books, 1983).

———, *The Unschooled Mind: How Children Think and How Schools Should Teach* (New York: Basic Books, 1991).

Daniel Goleman, *Emotional Intelligence* (New York: Bantam, 1995).

Ron Heifetz, *Leadership without Easy Answers* (Cambridge, MA: Harvard University Press, 1994).

Paul T. Hill, Lawrence C. Pierce, and James W. Guthrie, *Reinventing Public Education* (Chicago: University of Chicago Press, 1997).

Susan Moore Johnson, *Teachers at Work* (New York: Basic Books, 1990).

Robert Kegan and Lisa Laskow Lahey, *How the Way We Talk Can Change the Way We Work: Seven Languages for Transformation* (San Francisco: Jossey-Bass, 2000).

Deborah Meier, *The Power of Their Ideas* (Boston: Beacon Press, 1996).

Richard Murnane and Frank Levy, *Teaching the New Basic Skills* (New York: The Free Press, 1996).

Robert Putnam, *Bowling Alone: The Collapse and Revival of American Community* (New York: Simon & Schuster, 2000).

Richard Rothstein, *The Way We Were? The Myths and Realities of American Student Achievement* (New York: The Century Foundation Press, 1998).

Juliet Schor, *The Overworked American: The Unexpected Decline of Leisure* (New York: Basic Books, 1991).

Theodore R. Sizer, *Horace's School* (Boston: Houghton Mifflin, 1994).

Theodore R. Sizer and Nancy F. Sizer, *The Students Are Watching* (Boston: Beacon Press, 2000).

James Stigler and James Hiebert, *The Teaching Gap* (New York: The Free Press, 1999).

Richard Suskind, *A Hope in the Unseen: An American Odyssey from the Inner City to the Ivy League* (New York: Broadway Books, 1998).

Rabindranath Tagore, *Rabindranath Tagore, an Anthology*, ed. Krishna Dulta and Andrew Robinson (New York: St. Martin's Press, 1977).

Tony Wagner, *How Schools Change: Lessons from Three Communities Revisited* (New York: Routledge/Falmer, 2000).

George Wood, *A Time to Learn* (New York: Penguin, 1998).

Daniel Yankelovich, *Coming to Public Judgment: Making Democracy Work in a Complex World* (Syracuse, NY: Syracuse University Press, 1991).

———, *The Magic of Dialogue* (New York: Simon & Schuster, 1999).